DOLPHIN:

THE PERFECT GAMEFISH

DOLPHIN:
THE PERFECT GAMEFISH

Capt. Jim Sharpe

The Fisherman's International Publishing House
P.O. Box 421203
Summerland Key, FL 33042-1203

Editor . . . . Albia Dugger
Illustrator . . . . Dave Underwood
Photos . . . . Jim Sharpe
Cover . . . . Don Ray
Preface . . . . Jim Sharpe
Foreword . . . . Albia Dugger
Desk Top Publishing . . . . Anne O'Bannon

Publisher's Cataloging in Publishing

Sharpe, Capt. Jim (James)
    Dolphin: the perfect gamefish / by Capt. Jim Sharpe.
    p. cm.
    1. Perciformes. 2. Fishing. I. Title.
QL638.C795S43 1996   597'.58
                           QB196-40278

Txu 764-128
ISBN 1-889895-04-0

Dedication

To my wife Barbara, my son Jimmy and daughter Christina for their support during the long years it took to write this book. To Albia Dugger for her patience and for lending her scientific knowledge, experience and editing skills to organizing and communicating a life-time of learning. And to the memory of my father, who passed away when I was only seventeen, for teaching me to understand the ocean and for planting the seeds that guided the development of the fishing skills which I passed along to my son and daughter.

THE COVER

Artist Don Ray created this realistic painting of dolphin feeding in the Gulf Stream. Ray has spent most of his life developing a reputation as one of the world's finest painters of fresh and salt water fish. He strives to paint his subjects in as natural a setting as possible, studying the way light changes below the water's surface and using those effects to accurately represent the animals in their own environment.

Ray's paintings appear in many popular wildlife magazines and sporting catalogs including *"Field and Stream"*, *"Outdoor Life"*, *"Florida Sportsman"*, *"Ontario Out of Doors"*, *"Game Fish"* (France), *"Cabela's"*, *"Penn Reels"* and *"National Wildlife"* and on the cover of the International Game Fish Association's annual *"World Record Game Fishes"* book.

Attention to detail has won Ray several first-places in Florida State's Lobster Stamp and Snook Stamp competitions, as well as selection to paint the Coastal Conser-vation Association's 1994 stamp and print and the 1996-1997 Texas Saltwater Fishing stamp and print. He is a member of the Society of Animal Artists and has won the society's Award of Excellence.

To learn more about Don Ray's paintings call 561-388-2477.

Foreword

Dolphin fishing in the Florida Keys isn't as easy as it used to be in the days before electronics and high-powered engines made certain not even dolphin living in the open ocean can hide from fishermen's hooks. Now, it seems fish are becoming scarcer, smaller maybe even smarter. And, there's a lot more competition out there on the rip these days.

It used to be "good enough" to rely on luck alone to catch a nice dolphin for dinner, or to weigh in "the big one" to win a tournament. Now it takes specialized skill and knowledge as well.

If that's what you're looking for, you've found the right place. Not only has Capt. Jim Sharpe unlocked the secrets of dolphin behavior through 35 years of faithfully observing their feeding, schooling and migration habits from the bridge of a charter boat but he's added the results of every scientific research paper on the subject he could find, to cover all the bases. Then he puts it all together with seasonal and weather information, specific tips on using birds and baits as fishing signposts, plus detailed rigging and fishing techniques. The result: making sure you and I can predict dolphin migration and feeding patterns, and locate and catch dolphin, under every conceivable set of circumstances and conditions.

This book is not only the technical HOW TO, but the scientific WHY of dolphin fishing. The basic principles Capt. Sharpe sets forth for the Florida Keys should be valid throughout the world, everywhere dolphin are caught . For the first time, this book brings everything that makes dolphin "The Perfect Gamefish" together in one place but, let us keep the word "gamefish" as our guide. Use the information in this book to better the quality of your catch, not the quantity. Like Capt. Sharpe, practice catch-and-release and voluntary bag limits to make every fishing trip a success.

Albia Dugger, *Sport Fisheries Research*

Reference Wheel

I have developed a reference wheel called the "*Dolphin Fisherman's Crystal Ball*," to act as a quick, portable reference guide to the information in this book. It is water resistant and designed to be carried on the water. To use the "*Crystal Ball*," simply enter the wind direction and moon phase. The quick reference wheel pre-dicts dolphin feeding behavior and recommends the best fishing meth-od. It also predicts changes in the dolphin's feeding habits as the fishing day progresses and environmental factors change.

For more information, refer to *Appendix J.*

TABLE OF CONTENTS

K. Recommended references

Listing of drawings, pictures and illustrations

PART 1

DOLPHIN LIFE AND HABITS

Chapter I
Distribution, Migration And Feeding

In the Pacific waters off Hawaii they are called mahi-mahi. In the Caribbean they are called dorado. In the Western Atlantic from the Florida Keys to the Outer Banks of the Carolinas they're called dolphin.

Neon-colored gamefish, dolphin thrill anglers with their non-stop jumping, tailwalking and head-thrashing attempts to throw the hook. Favorites not only for their great fighting ability but for their excellent table fare, dolphin make colorful wall trophies for anglers wanting to preserve their memories.

Unique in its shape, agility and ability to change color, a dolphin in the water is typically a rich iridescent Caribbean blue or blue-green dorsally, depending on water color. Its lower flanks are bluish-green with shades of gold or silver, sprinkled with a mixture of light, iridescent blue spots, while the belly shades to silvery white or yellow.

The very nature of the dolphin makes it a great gamefish, feeding at or near the surface, schooling in large numbers around flotsam and jetsam, and leaping into the air when threatened by predators or hook-and-line.

Dolphin: The Perfect Gamefish

1. The "Pompano Dolphin" and the "Common Dolphin"

There are two separate species of dolphin: the pompano dolphin ("*Coryphaena equiselis*") and the common dolphin ("*Coryphaena hippurus*"). The pompano dolphin, the smaller and more oceanic of the two species, is quickly distinguished from the common dolphin by its shape. In pompano dolphin, the greatest body depth is near the

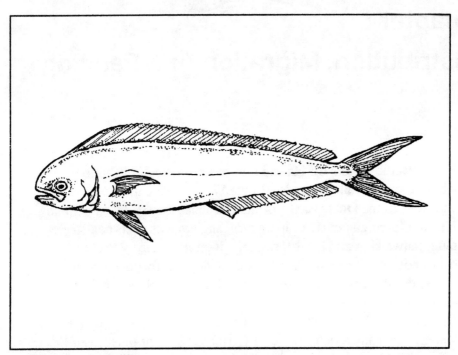

1. Common Dolphin

middle of the body instead of up front, close to the head, as in common dolphin. The pectoral fins of the pompano dolphin are much smaller and the dorsal fin is much fuller and shorter, originating behind the eye rather than directly above the eye as in the common dolphin. Also, the anal fin of the pompano dolphin is convex, while the anal fin of the common dolphin is concave.

Dolphin have no spines in any of the fins. The dorsal fin of the common dolphin has 55 to 66 soft rays, the concave anal fin has 25 to 31 soft rays and there are 31 vertebrae.

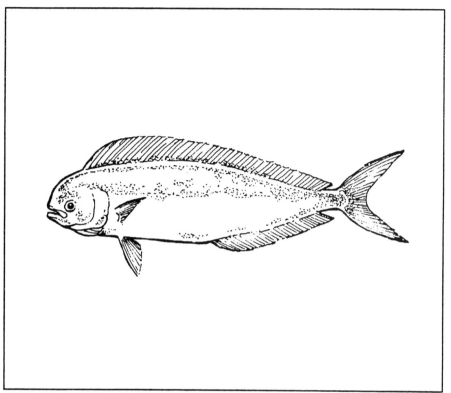

2. Pompano Dolphin

dorsal fin of the pompano dolphin has 52 to 59 soft rays, the convex anal fin has 23 to 29 rays and there are 33 vertebrae. (See: Appendix I, Dolphin Fins)

"2. Distribution"

There are apparently two stocks of dolphin, one occurring above and one occurring below the equator. In the western Atlantic, common dolphin have been reported as far north as George's Bank, Nova Scotia ("Vladykov and McKenzie 1935; Tibbo 1962") and as far south as Rio de Janeiro, Brazil ("Ribeiro, 1918; Shcherbachev, 1973").

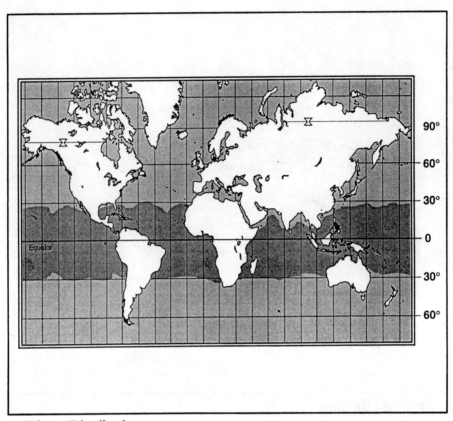

3. Winter Distribution

In the Atlantic, dolphin are most abundant off Puerto Rico in February and March.

In the Pacific, dolphin make up 93 to 96 percent of the total catch in the "Shiira-zuke" fishery during the season running from June to October.

In East African waters common dolphin are caught from November to June, with March to May being the most abundant months.

Common dolphin are widely distributed in the Mediterranean with the dolphin becoming most abundant August to November.

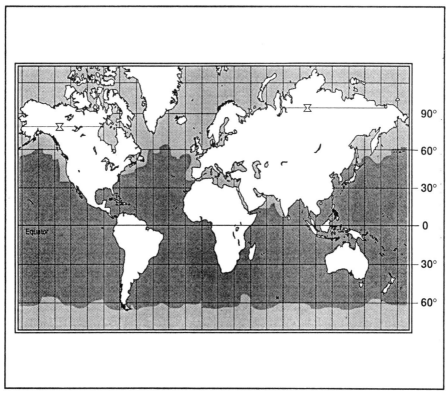

4. Summer Distribution

"3. Temperature and Migration"

There is very little published information about migrations of either common or pompano dolphin. Dolphin tagging has not provided much information due to the fact that most tagged dolphin are recovered within 10 days of being tagged.

Most fishery scientists would agree, however, that dolphin in the northern hemisphere migrate north from the equator during the spring and summer then return south (toward the equator) in the fall.

These seasonal migrations correspond with warming surface water temperatures that dolphin prefer and the migration of baitfish. The key to understanding the migration of the dolphin is their affinity for certain water temperatures.

Isotherms are areas of the ocean with the same surface water temperatures, symbolized on charts by a series of lines drawn on the ocean surface. Dolphin movements and migrations can be accurately predicted by observing these isotherms and applying their known water temperature preferences.

Dolphin: The Perfect Gamefish

In a report, "*Synopsis of the Biological Data on Dolphin*", NOAA Technical Report NMFS Circular 443, April 1982, studies showed that dolphin are generally year-round residents in oceans or gulfs where surface water temperatures remain above 78.8° Fahrenheit (26° Celsius) and the 0- to 100-foot depth is clear and blue.

Pronounced seasonal variations in abundance and distribution were reported where surface water temperatures fell below 78.8° Fahrenheit at certain times of the year. This report further stated that, in general, common dolphin did not occur in waters where surface temperatures were below 69.8° Fahrenheit (21° Celsius). One exception was noted near the Philippine Islands in the Sea of Japan, in waters adjacent to Eastern Taiwan and the northeastern part of Batan Islands where dolphin were reported along the 18° to 19° Celsius isotherm. These dolphin were thought to be traveling through these waters to reach warmer currents.

The more oceanic pompano dolphin were found only where surface temperatures were above 75.2° Fahrenheit (24° Celsius) and are most common in the waters off Hawaii. Common dolphin have a greater area of distribution during migrations due to wider tolerances of surface temperature.

As warm water expands north and south from the equator with summer the dolphin follow the 78.8° to 82.4° Fahrenheit (26° to 28° Celsius) isotherms (areas of constant mean temperatures). In the Northern and Southern Hemispheres the different stocks of dolphin move away from the equator following the isotherms, extending their distribution north and south as the oceans warm.

Dolphin reach their greatest distribution with the warm waters of summer. As winter approaches and the water cools, the dolphin retreat following the isotherms back into the tropical waters surrounding the equator to spend the winter.

"4. Spring and Fall Migration"

The spring migration, moving away from the equatorial zone between lattitudes (24° N and 24° S) is made up primarily of juvenile feeding schools accompanied by a few larger adult dolphin, both bulls and cows. After feeding and growing throughout the summer, dolphin in the fall migration form primarily spawning schools, adult schools, and pods or "wolf packs" of mature dolphin.

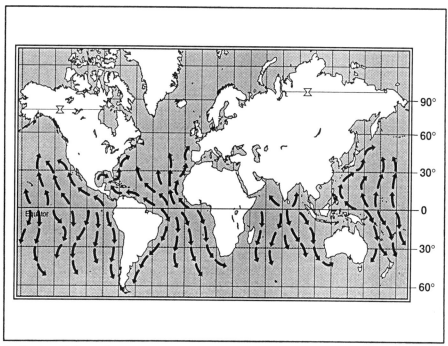

5. Spring Migration

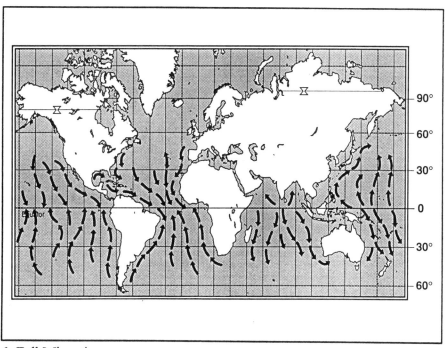

6. Fall Migration

Chapter II
Biology

1. "Bulls and Cows"

Mature male and female dolphin look different. Male dolphin, called bulls, are larger than females and have high, vertical foreheads. Females, or cows, are smaller and have rounded foreheads which slope gently with a slow radius toward the dorsal fin.

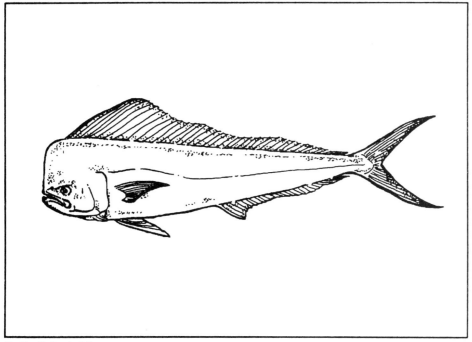

7. Bull Dolphin

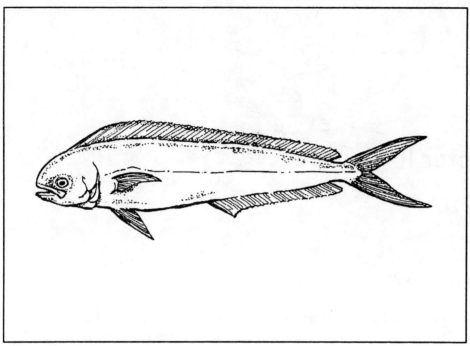

8. Cow Dolphin

2. "Age and Growth"

Dolphin growth is very rapid in warm water. With a plentiful food supply, dolphin can reach most of their genetic growth potential in less than two years.

Dr. Grant Beardsley of the University of Miami ("*1967*") reported that a 1-pound male dolphin placed into a large tank at the Miami Seaquarium grew to 32 pounds in eight months. The Miami Herald ("*1961*") reported that two common dolphin at Marineland, Florida, grew from one pound to 32 and 37 pounds, respectively, in 7½ and a half months. A 22-inch dolphin would be approximately 60 to 90 days old.

Dolphin mature in a matter of two months and have a very short life span, rarely living more than four years. Beardsley found that approximately 75 percent of dolphin he studied were less than one year old, and 98 percent were less than two years old. Less than 2 percent reached the third or fourth year.

Dolphin begin to mature at about 14 inches (350 mm) in length, becoming fully mature at 21 inches (550 mm) when they move on to the next social step of their lives in the ocean.

3. "Spawning and reproduction"

Dolphin prefer spawning at night in the top 0 to 10 meters (0 to 35 feet) of clear blue surface waters with temperatures of 78.8° to 82.4° Fahrenheit (26° to 28° Celsius), and lower salinities around 31 parts per thousand. (Average salinity is 28 to 39 parts per thousand).

Fertilization is external as male and female dolphin swim side by side, often accompanied by one to three other dolphin. The fertilized eggs of the common dolphin are buoyant, colorless and spherical, measuring 1.2 to 1.6 millimeters in diameter, with a single yellow oil globule measuring 0.3 to 0.4 millimeters in diameter.

A 16-pound female produces a total of 250,000 to 3,000,000 eggs each year in an average of three spawnings. The eggs develop and hatch into larvae within 60 hours in the warm water. The larvae are 15 millimeters in length at 15 days and appear brown in color. At this point the blunt snout and distinct fins are already present.

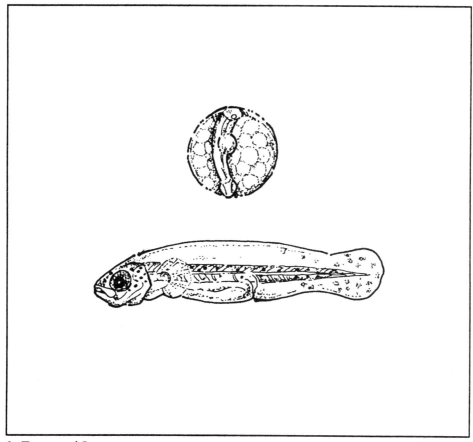

9. Eggs and Larvae

Dolphin: The Perfect Gamefish

The eggs and larvae of the pompano and common dolphin are very similar until they reach the juvenile stage, after which they can be easily identified by color patterns. Juvenile pompano dolphin tend to be uniformly dark on the sides. Juvenile common dolphin appear brown with alternating dark and light vertical bars resembling a feather, with this pattern often continuing into the fins. This vertical pattern of bars can be seen in larger dolphin during aggressive feeding.

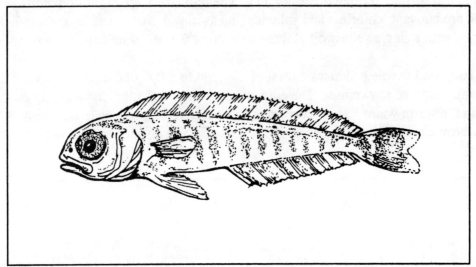

10. Juvenile Common Dolphin

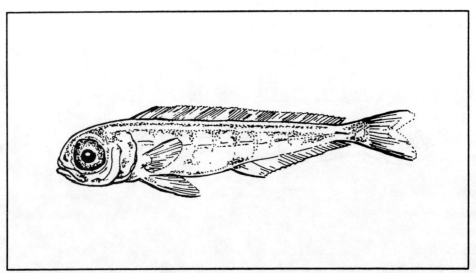

11. Juvenile Pompono Dolphin

4. "Spawning Seasons"

Dolphin spawn year-round in warm climates like the Florida Current with peak spawning periods in January, February and March (*"Beardsley, 1967"*). Dolphin born off the Florida Keys will mature and spawn by the end of the summer as they begin their southerly migration.

Off North Carolina, spawning is most intense during June and July in the Gulf Stream (*"Gibbs and Collette, 1959; Beardsley, 1967; Shcherbachev, 1973; Fahay, 1975"*). Off Ocean City, Maryland, Gibbs and Collette found dolphin ready to spawn in July and August.

In the Pacific off southern Japan, the common dolphin spawns in July and August (*"Okada, 1955"*).

Record Catches

A 25- to 30-pound dolphin is considered a trophy-size fish because larger dolphin are rare. However, dolphin can grow to 100 pounds or more. Florida Sportsman magazine reported a dolphin of 101 pounds captured off the coast of Puerto Rico in 1979. Here are some other examples of world-class dolphin caught by fishermen in the Florida Keys and around the world. Angler Manuel Salazar landed the existing IGFA all-tackle world record 87-pound-test off Costa Rica in Septemper, 1976. A lady angler caught a larger dolphin, weighing 89 pounds, off Islamorda, Florida but the catch was not entered as a record because more than one angler fought the fish.

In May, 1991 at our Sea Boots Marina, Summerland Key, Florida angler Sue Anderson weighted in a women's world record dolphin weighting 68 pounds, caught on 80-pound-test line. That record was beaten in 1993 with an 82-pound dolphin caught off Cabo San Lucas Mexico.

Although not a world record, angler Kathleen Teague landed a 72-pound bull dolphin on 20-pound test while fishing aboard the charter boat Sun Dance off Big Pine in the Florida Keys with Capt. Paul Horton. The standing women's world record on 20-pound test line, an 83-pounder, was caught off Cabo San Lucas, Mexico, in 1972.

World record catches in the fly-fishing division are equally impressive. Veteran fly angler Stu Apte caught a 58-pound bull on 12-pound-test tippet in Piñas Bay, Panama in 1964.

World records are constantly changing as old records are broken and new records are established. For an updated record, contact the International Game Fish Association in Pompano, Florida.

12. Angler Kathleen Teague with her seventy-two pound bull dolphin

Chapter III
Dolphin Behavior

1. "Schooling and Social Order of Dolphin"

In order to fully understand the schooling and social order of dolphin, let's follow the school structure as young fish pass through various stages. First, dolphin join juvenile feeding schools, then progress to adult spawning schools. In the off-spawning period, adult feeding schools segregate by sex and size. Finally there are smaller pods of fully mature bulls and cows known as "wolf packs."

<u>Juvenile feeding schools:</u> Dolphin belong first to juvenile feeding schools, which contain the greatest number of small individuals (100 to 200 fish per school, averaging from two to six pounds each), both male and female. These young dolphin are at great risk from predators. Lacking the greater strength and agility of the larger adult fish, they find surviving and feeding easier in large schools.

Schools of fish react as one . When predators attack, the entire school can turn instantaneously or take flight by greyhounding across the surface in a rapid series of jumps. Scientists now believe schooling fish emit a pulse type of sound wave instructing the entire school which way to dart to escape danger.

A single fish in the feeding school will occasionally leap from the water and turn on their side to strike the water's surface, creating a loud sound to help other school members track the location of the school.

Schools form around objects floating at the surface of the ocean and will return to the object and reform the school after predators or anglers attack them.

Dolphin: The Perfect Gamefish

Juvenile feeding schools are often accompanied by several large dolphin which cannibalize the smaller fish when food becomes scarce or an opportunity presents.

Off the Florida Keys, feeding schools are common in May as the young fish begin their migration northward along Florida's east coast.

Adult spawning schools: Dolphin in adult spawning schools usually run from eight to 22 pounds (Size increases from early summer to late summer). Feeding and survival are still good reasons for schooling but spawning is far more important at this stage of their lives. These dolphin are from 90 days to 180 days old; that's middle age in a dolphin's life.

Dolphins are heterosexual and pair off in the school for spawning. These schools are most often seen in the Western Atlantic along the east coast of Florida from the Florida Keys to the Carolina's in mid-to late summer.

13. Schooling Dolphin

Adult feeding schools: Dolphin school by size and sex. During the off spawning cycle it is not unusual to find schools of adult dolphin ranging in size from eight to 22 pounds that are mostly female. These concentrations of fish are closely associated with tidal rips and weedlines along the continental shelf. The males prefer the solitude of the open ocean farther offshore then return to the adult spawning schools during season.

Wolf packs of large dolphin: The final stage of dolphin life is called a pod or "wolf pack" made up of 2 to 6 fish, usually one or two bulls and several cows, ranging in size from 20 to more than 45 pounds. The bulls are usually larger than the cows in the groups. These fish are extremely agile, strong and able to escape most predators with ease with the exception of the blue marlin. Large dolphin roaming in wolf packs often feed on smaller feeding schools of dolphin, finding them easy prey.

I have observed schools of 10 to 20 dolphin ranging from 20 to 35 pounds feeding on weedlines or schooling under flotsam in late August along the Florida Keys.

2. "Flotsam, Jetsam and Navigation"

Dolphin's attraction to Flotsam and Jetsam: Dolphin have a particular attraction for objects found on or near the surface including boards, sea turtles, whale sharks, logs and patches of seaweed. Given the clarity of offshore water, these objects are very visible to dolphin from the surface to 100-foot depths where they spend most of their time.

Objects on the surface serve as a central point where young dolphin can gather into schools. Most dolphin spend their larval and juvenile stages darting in and out of seaweed patches and around other floating objects that offer food and protection from predators.

The dolphin's attraction to surface objects seems to go beyond providing food. These objects act as schooling companions, navigational points of reference and offer visual stimulation in an otherwise optical void. Dolphin have been known to follow sailboats or towed vessels for hundreds of miles. At certain times of the year, dolphin are known to follow turtles and whale sharks.

Navigation: I have observed the dolphin's uncanny ability to locate and sense direction of objects floating on the ocean's surface. Although neither I nor the experts understand the dolphin's navigational abilities fully, I would like to offer some observations.

Dolphin: The Perfect Gamefish

One beautiful calm July day about 20 miles south of Key West, while charter fishing on board the "Sea Boots" we encountered a large log. As we approached the log I yelled to the mate to get ready. The water under this log was blue with dolphin of all sizes. As we passed the log, which was floating almost sub-surface, several large bulls greyhounded in behind the baits and the fight was on. I pulled the "Sea Boots" into neutral and we enjoyed some spectacular dolphin fishing.

After catching and releasing as many of the sporty game fish as our party could physically stand, we just drifted along watching the schooled dolphin swim back and forth under the boat.

With no bait in the water the dolphin soon got bored and one by one began to swim away – all in the same direction. I wondered, could they sense the direction of the log? The surface of the ocean was like a mirror and I could watch the dolphin swimming away for quite a distance. Suddenly it dawned on me that I could no longer see the log; we had drifted quite some distance from it. I took a compass course on the dolphin swimming away and followed that compass course about 500 yards right back to the log.

14. Flotsam and Jetsam

18

Chapter IV
Food and Feeding Habits

1. "Feeding Habits"

Dolphin feed in the top 100 feet of the water column regardless of the depth of the water. Hydrodynamically designed for speed and agility, dolphin can reach speeds in excess of 50 miles per hour, enabling them to catch jumping surface prey such as flying fish. Their flattened shape enables them to roll onto their sides to pass close under boards or seaweed to catch small prey.

Many anglers think dolphin are always found feeding around weedlines, flotsam and jetsam – but this isn't necessarily so. There are many times of year when dolphin don't come to the weedlines but will chase bait in the open water a half-mile away. There are also many times of year dolphin will not congregate under flotsam such as boards or other floating debris.

Dolphin have a range of feeding patterns that change during the year – from the top of the reef in November to the far reaches of the blue water in late summer feeding at night on a full moon, below the surface due to cool surface temperatures, under boards or sargassum, or in the open blue water along rips or under birds.

Dolphin simply respond to the most abundant food source. When flying fish or other baitfish are abundant in the open expanses of blue-water, and in short supply under flotsam, you will find schools of dolphin pursuing them.

When deciding where to fish for dolphin, the experienced blue water angler sizes up the fishing conditions on a day-by-day basis, considering the migrational habits at the time of year, moon phase, recent weather conditions, wind direction, tides, currents and the position of the Gulf Stream.

2. "Dolphin Diets"

The dolphin's diet changes as it grows. Juvenile dolphin feed mainly on crustaceans, particularly copepods which make vertical migrations and concentrate near the surface at night. As dolphin grow older, their diet consists of roughly 25 percent flying fish and 25 percent squid, the remainder of the diet is comprised of mackerel and many varieties of small fish that dwell under flotsam and jetsam.

Dolphin by necessity become opportunistic feeders in late summer or early winter, when food gets scarce. Then dolphin will come to the edge of the reef to feed on ballyhoo or turn to alternative sources of food.

I have learned a great deal about gamefish feeding habits over the years by observing their stomach contents. On many occasions I've felt something like a hair brush inside a dolphin's stomach. Upon opening the stomach I found a lump of sargassum seaweed and small yellow sea horses. Apparently they find it too time consuming to pick each sea horse out of the seaweed, so they just eat the sea horses, seaweed and all. I have found small sailfish, swordfish and even small dolphin that have fallen prey to the ravenous appetites of other dolphin. Other captains have observed birds (white egrets), plastic parts of underarm deodorant sticks, and even chicken bones in dolphin stomachs.

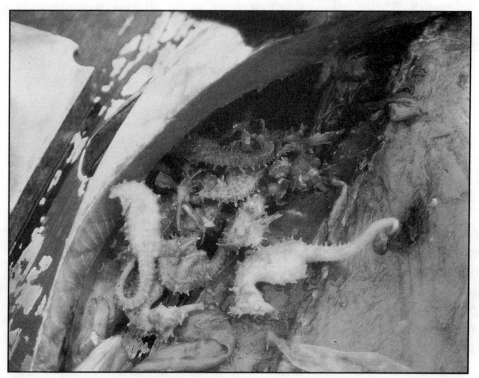

15. Sea Horses, Stomach Content

Stomach contents can give the angler a lot of information on where the fish are feeding. Flying fish would indicate surface feeding, squid would indicate sub-surface or nocturnal feeding. Small file fish or jack fish would indicate feeding under grass or boards.

16. Sea Horses, Stomach Content

3. "Prey Size"

One of the most important elements of dolphin fishing is the size of the bait (either artificial or natural). Common dolphin world-wide seem to prefer flying fish, the species most often found in their stomachs. Pompano dolphin, however, seem to prefer crustaceans, particularly in the Pacific and Indian Oceans (*"Shcherbachev, 1973"*).

In the western Sea of Japan, samples of stomach contents of 1,103 adult common dolphin ranging from 14 to 40 inches in length revealed two basic size ranges of food. Eighty-five percent of their diet consisted of fish ranging from 1 to 34 centimeters (½ to 12 inches), which were in turn divided into two primary size groups: 2 to 4 centimeters (1 to 1½ inches) and 10 to 15 centimeters (4 to 6 inches).

These figures are consistent with my own observations and should send a strong message to the angler purchasing artificial lures or bait to troll for dolphin.

17. Baitfish, Stomach Content

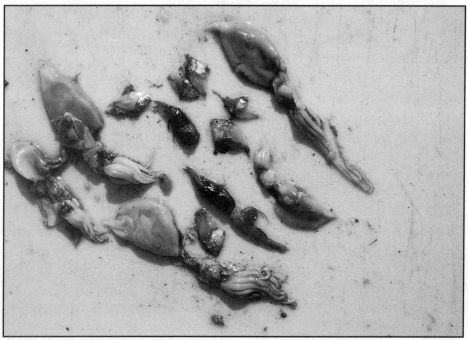

18. Stomach Content, Squid

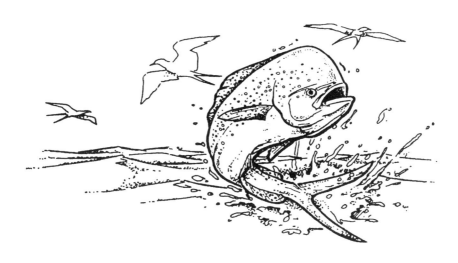

PART 2

ENVIRONMENTAL INFLUENCES

Chapter V
Changing Winds

1. "Ideal Conditions"

How do dolphin react to the direction of the wind, changes in weather and the phase of the moon? Dolphin are very sensitive to changes in their environment, including weather changes (upper-level low-pressure areas, etc.) and wind direction; water salinity, clarity and temperature; and direction and strength of current. Knowing how dolphin will react to factors that change daily and influence their behavior, the dolphin fisherman can fairly accurately predict how the fish will bite and where.

There are many factors at work in the ocean that influence growth and abundance of the species and, unfortunately, only a relative few that we understand. Dolphin, although very adaptable to changing environments, seem to flourish under certain conditions. I have already mentioned some of the conditions that dolphin consider ideal: Warm water (78.8° to 82.4° Fahrenheit), salinity (32.00/00 to 36.00/00), and clear blue water surface water (0 to 100 feet).

2. "Wind Direction"

Wind direction is one of the primary factors determining successful or unsuccessful dolphin fishing trips. In general, wind direction combined with other factors determines the development of favorable or non-favorable feeding conditions.

In April, for example, easterly winds bring favorable feeding conditions for dolphin, concentrating bait in 300 to 500 feet of water and bringing warm surface temperatures. On the other hand, northeast winds disperse bait and cool surface temperatures, discouraging surface feeding.

During June, southeasterly trade winds, combined with strong northerly current in the Gulf Stream, concentrate the abundant sargassum seaweed into long, straight lines paralleling the current. These weedlines are perfect conditions for large concentrations of bait and dolphin. In general, dolphin prefer winds in the southeasterly quadrant of the compass, from 90° to 180°.

On an easterly wind, dolphin will sometimes tail, producing a different feeding pattern. On this wind, special techniques must be used to get the dolphin to bite, particularly if the wind is over 15 knots.

On a more southerly wind, dolphin will school on weedlines or boards and feed very aggressively.

3. "Tailing Dolphin"

In the southern part of the Florida Keys, a strong east-northeast wind, parallel to shore, will cause dolphin to tail. Tailing is a term used to describe fish using the circular, upper-surface cyclonic movement of wave energy to propel them into the strong flow of the Gulf Stream current (*Illustration 37*).

In the middle and upper Keys, the current flows in a more northerly direction and dolphin will tail on a northeast wind. The important factor is that the wind is opposing the flow of the current when tailing begins – a principle which can be applied in many parts of the world. As dolphin migrate northward along the east coast of the United States, north and northeast winds create tailing conditions wherever the wind opposes the flow of the current.

Dolphin in this feeding mode will cruise near the surface, feeding mainly on flying fish. These fish want a fast-moving bait – one that presents a challenge to catch – and fight like tigers once hooked.

On a northeast wind the dolphin will tail if surface baitfish are available (flying fish or ballyhoo). Often located under birds, tailing fish are difficult to attract to anything but live bait or sight-casted baits splashed nearby.

4. "Lock-Jaw on Northerly Winds"

When the wind shifts to the north and northeast, dolphin take on an attitude about biting: You could call it "lock-jaw," when fish refuse to surface-feed and stay well below the surface. (Northerly winds break up weedlines and surface concentrations.) They react similarly to tailing fish but need a lot of motivation to feed and are quite often caught only on the deep troll.

Under these conditions, an angler could go offshore fishing for dolphin and simply rent the bait and turn it in at the end of the fishing day. Many anglers come to the charter boat docks on a spring day preceding a cold front moving down the state. These light southerly winds just before the front produce excellent dolphin fishing conditions and the catches reflect that fact.

Our angler, now enthused by the catch, returns the next day after the winds have shifted with the front to the north, finds that the dolphin suddenly have lock-jaw. The northerly winds have dispersed the weedlines and broken up surface conditions that produced the dolphin action.

A couple days after the cold front passes the winds will shift back to the east. The magic switch for the dolphin is that point where the compass reaches the 90° mark, entering the more productive southerly quadrant (90° to 180°).

Effects of a Northeast Wind

Many years ago, when I was still looking for proof of the wind's effects on fish off the Keys, I just happened to be floating along a weedline in 800 feet of water with a moderate east wind. This weedline was a dolphin angler's dream. The sargassum seaweed was lined up in a straight line to the horizon – as far as the eye could see – 20 feet wide with three feet of vertical development. Vertical development is an important factor in weedlines as it vastly increases the amount of baitfish, shrimp and crabs the floating mass holds.

Many logs and boards were entwined in the weedline and, of course, there were multiple schools of dolphin of all sizes, aggressively feeding.

At noon, a strengthening high off Cape Hatteras began to shift the wind off the Keys from east back to the northeast. As the wind passed north of the 90 degree mark on the compass to east-northeast, the dolphin were still visible under the dispersing weedline but feeding slowed, then stopped altogether as the weedline continued to break up.

---

5. "Southerly winds"

A southerly wind, combined with a strong northerly flow of the Gulf Stream, tends to develop weedlines of sargassum seaweed and flotsam such as boards or other debris (*Illustration 23*).

Dolphin: The Perfect Gamefish

Major weedline development generally occurs from mid-June to late August along the east coast of United States. Dolphin in this feeding mode generally mill around floating debris feeding on small baitfish (file fish, small jack etc.) or swim along under the weedlines, feeding on small baitfish. These fish are not as aggressive fighters as the tailing fish on the east winds but give the angler a thrilling airborne fight that is characteristic of the dolphin.

Wind and Bonus Years

After observing the dolphin season over a period of 30 years it became apparent to me that bonus years (years with more and larger dolphin than average) seem to occur every three or four years. The amount of wind during the pre-spawning months in the Florida Current (January, February and March) seemed to be a key factor in the bonus years.

The wind stirs the water, distributing algae (phytoplankton) to greater depths in the water column. The algae is the main food source of copepods (small crustaceans). The greater distribution of algae in turn increases the distribution and amount of copepods, which are the main food source of juvenile dolphin. With an abundant food resource the dolphin increase in number and size creating the bonus year.

The year 1989 was one of those bonus years for big dolphin along the Florida Keys. In February and March, a strong southeast wind blew along the Keys for 45 days, rarely dropping below 25 knots. At this time, juvenile dolphin born in the Florida Current along the Lower Keys and Key West were developing. As we moved into summer and the wind shifted to the south in late April, the school dolphin were noticeably heavier than normal and were more abundant. By mid- to late-summer increased numbers of 50- to 60-pound dolphin were landed along the Keys.

Note: This theory is based on research conducted by Ronald E. Thresher of the CSIRO Marine Laboratory on the abundance of Scott's weedfish ("Heteroclinus" sp.) in the waters off southeastern Tasmania, which indicated wind was a great factor in stimulating abundant numbers and larger average sizes of weedfish.

Chapter VI
Currents and Tides

1. "Ocean Highways"

Coastal tides and warm-water currents in tropical and sub-tropical oceans around the world are the highways that dolphin travel. Dolphin seek out these currents and read them like a navigational chart. They swim into the flow of the current as winter approaches to find the warm waters of the equatorial zone. Then they swim with the current when summer returns, following the isotherms north and south from the equatorial zone.

The Gulf Stream, an immense river of water some 35 to 45 miles wide, flowing from the Florida Straits northward along Florida's east coast toward North Carolina, then bending northeast toward Europe, is an excellent example of one of these dolphin highways. This warm current flows at a velocity of 2 to 6 knots and averages a warm 79°F. Associated with the Gulf Stream are smaller counter currents, eddies and meanders that spin off from the main flow of the Gulf Stream.

Tides result from the gravitational effects of the sun and moon on the water's surface, resulting in high and low tides that flow in and out of the inland bays and channels and effect the nearshore waters of the ocean, within 25 miles of shore. Coastal currents and tides vary in volume with the phases of the moon producing a profound effect on dolphin feeding activity.

2. "The Gulf Stream"

The term "Gulf Stream" is one of the most misunderstood in fishing language. Most anglers see the Gulf Stream as a large area of blue water just offshore of the reef. However, it's important to understand some basic concepts.

The Gulf Stream begins in the equatorial trade winds. As the trade winds blow across the water from east to west, a force is applied to its surface at an oblique angle to the wind resulting in a northerly flow of current. Numerous currents from the Caribbean and the Gulf of Mexico merge with the Gulf Stream in the Florida Straits, then begin to flow north, averaging from 2 to 6 knots.

As the water of the Gulf Stream enters the Mid-Atlantic, the water cools, gradually sinking to the bottom where it begins to flow south, replacing the northerly flow. To realize the magnitude of the Gulf Stream current, picture a block of water averaging more than 1,000 feet deep, 40 miles wide and 4 miles long, passing by you each hour.

This mighty river is not one continuous flow of current. It is comprised of a number of currents moving at different velocities within its entirety. Like fingers, these currents produce rips and eddies along the edge of their flow gathering flotsam and jetsam that may draw schooling dolphin. It is extremely important to understand the nature of these currents and how dolphin use them.

3. "Counter-Currents"

The term counter-current as applied to the Florida Keys and the southeastern coast of Florida refers to a current produced by the northerly flow of the powerful Gulf Stream. The counter-current is not a constant flow, but flows from time to time in an opposing direction, close to the reef, generally extending from 1 mile offshore out to 350 feet of water.

Ships traveling south can save fuel by using the counter-currents, flowing at 1 to 2 knots, rather than fighting the strong flow of the Gulf Stream. Counter-currents have a very positive effect on the seas outside the reef during the predominantly easterly winds of winter. Northerly flow of the Gulf Stream into the easterly winds produces large seas, but the southerly flow of the counter-current with the wind has a calming effect. (Note: The Gulf Stream flows east along the Lower

Keys and Key West turning northeast at Islamorada, then north as it reaches Miami.)

The counter-current varies with the position and velocity of the Gulf Stream, pulling water southward along its edge. Rips can develop along the edge of the counter-current where it meets the Gulf Stream, concentrating bait, flotsam and jetsam and, with the right conditions, produce lots of dolphin action.

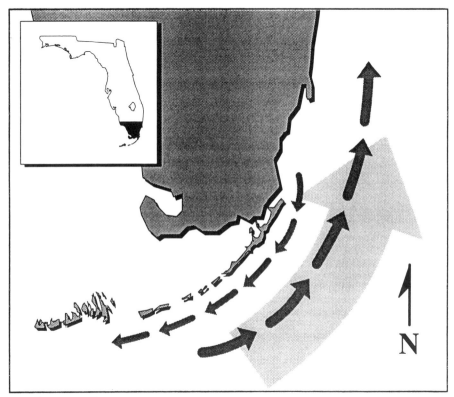

19. Counter Current

4. "Meanders"

Meanders are currents, perhaps several miles wide, originating from the main Gulf Stream current, that simply meander, taking no certain course. Meanders resemble a long, winding snake and can form rips and eddies along their edges, attracting many species of gamefish. But, for the dolphin fisherman, the most important aspect is the strong rips and eddies which concentrate flotsam and jetsam (such as boards and sargassum) along their edges, forming excellent dolphin surface-feeding conditions.

I have made a couple of very interesting observations about rips along the edge of meanders: First, rips running parallel with the flow of the Gulf Stream produce the best dolphin action. Second, rips running across the Gulf Stream produce the best wahoo action.

I would guess that the rips running with the current have very limited temperature changes and the rips crossing the normal flow of the current have much greater temperature changes. Dolphin are very sensitive to cooler water, but wahoo prefer it. Modern infra-red, surface-monitoring weather satellites can give accurate data during the winter on the location of the Gulf Stream and existing eddies and meanders.

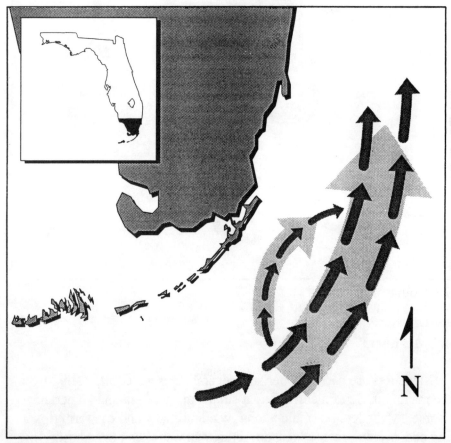

20. Meander

5. "Eddies"

Eddies are circular, spinning masses of water which develop along the edges of the Gulf Stream. These can be quite large, measuring more than 10 miles across. Eddies concentrate nutrients, bait, flotsam and jetsam and, ultimately, gamefish. These large, swirling masses of water can produce excellent swordfishing, attract pods of whales and concentrate schools of dolphin under boards or large patches of sargassum seaweed that get trapped in the eddy.

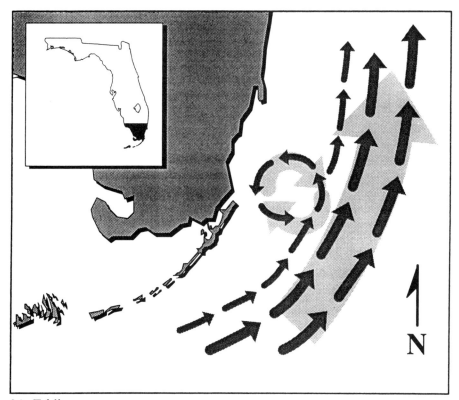

21. Eddies

6. "Upwelling Cold Water Currents"

Tidal volume increases as the moon nears the full or new moon phases, and the Gulf Stream begins to swell, expanding in width. As the shoreward edge of the Gulf Stream moves toward the edge of the

Dolphin: The Perfect Gamefish

continental shelf (15 miles offshore in 600 feet of water) it traps a large volume of water between the shoreward edge of the stream and the slope of the continental shelf.

This trapped water is forced upward, or upwelling. The result is an offshore surface run-off of the cool upwelling water being displaced. This usually lasts only one or two days, usually a few days before the full or new moon.

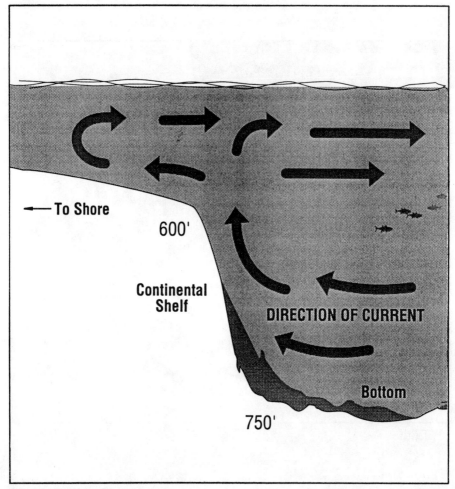

22. Upwelling Currents

The Force of the Gulf Stream

The force of the Gulf Stream is difficult to measure far at sea, but occasionally when these powerful currents move close to the reef their magnitude can be seen.

Many years ago, the late Dr. Gilbert Voss of the University of Miami Rosenstiel School of Marine and Atmospheric Science was called to investigate a fish kill off Fort Lauderdale, Florida. Arriving in the area just outside the reef in 100 feet of water, Dr. Voss found numerous fish floundering helplessly on the surface. The fish were mostly bottom dwellers: grouper and snapper. Samples were collected. The fish were tested and found to be negative for any red tide or toxins common to most fish kills.

Dr. Voss noted a very strong current that day along the reef and measured the speed of that current with a transit, shooting back to the shoreline. The analysis of the data gathered that day was very interesting. The tidal flow measurements showed that the Gulf Stream, extremely close to the reef that day, was flowing at an astonishing 10 knots. Dr. Voss estimated that the strong upwelling currents along the reef simply jetted the bottom-dwelling fish up fast enough to cause an embolus in their swim bladders.

I have personally witnessed the sea buoy at Government Cut in Miami pulled almost underwater by the powerful inshore edge of the Gulf Stream.

The Force of the Gulf Stream

7. "Tides"

The moon's gravitation exerts approximately 90 percent of the tidal pull on the earth. The alignment of the sun and moon during the new moon (neap tide) and their opposition in the full moon (flood tide) is responsible for the greatest tidal volume.

Dolphin: The Perfect Gamefish

Aggressive dolphin feeding takes place during periods of greater tidal volume. Tides flowing inshore (incoming tides) build toward the high tide and tides flowing offshore (outgoing tides) terminate with the low tide. Slack tide, or change of the tide, takes approximately thirty minutes and the same tide will occur approximately one hour later each day. (This is important to note because fish may bite one hour later each day when the same conditions are reached.) These tidal influences are not noticable offshore but pass like a giant wave as the gravitational forces move past.

For me, one of the most astounding discoveries in blue-water fishing was the realization that these tides have a tremendous effect on surface conditions more than 20 miles offshore. The blue-water angler should be armed with the times of the high and low tides when he starts offshore in search of dolphin. I often passed areas of scattered sargassum seaweed on an incoming tide, not realizing that, later in the day when the tide was out going, this same area of scattered weed would be pushed together into a tight weedline, potentially producing lots of dolphin action.

8. "Weedlines"

Outgoing tide exerts pressure on one side of the sargassum and the predominant southeasterly trade winds of summer push in the opposite direction on the other side, compacting the sargassum into a line called a weedline.

Weedlines and color changes move inshore (into shallower water) with the incoming tide and offshore (into deeper water) with the outgoing tide. This is important because changes in water depth, depending on surface conditions, will determine what variety of gamefish will be in the area.

23. Current and wind combine to form a weedline, composed of sargassum seaweed.

Chapter VII
Light and Weather

1. "Moon Phase"

We have already discussed the positive effect of the new and full moons as they relate to tidal volume, setting up rips and eddies and concentrating flotsam and jetsam. However, dolphin feeding also changes two to three days before the full moon when the brightest nights occur.

Dolphin may seem aggressive at first but quickly turn off, refusing to bite after several fish are caught from a school. Big dolphin will often charge a bait and swirl on it but not eat the bait during this period.

It's difficult to explain why dolphin react this way. During the bright nights of the full moon, tidal conditions are best at night and I believe the dolphin feed aggressively during the night. There is one positive note here: The dolphin will generally feed after 4:00 p.m. in the afternoon on the bright moon.

2. "Light and Barometric Pressure"

Dolphin also react to weather. Associated with some weather systems is a reduction of light and barometric pressure. Reduction of light is a very important factor in the dolphin's view. Dolphin very definitely do not like upper level, non-tropical low pressure areas that bring those gray skies and reduced light in the upper level of the water column.

These can be very slight weather changes. Sometimes the angler notices no change in wind direction or temperature. Since dolphin hunt prey mainly in the upper part of the water column, this reduction in light is a big factor to them and will slow the dolphin feeding to zero.

Weather that brings undesirable wind directions or cooler weather, dropping surface temperatures, will also shut down dolphin activity. Barometric changes associated with weather systems that do not reduce light can stimulate dolphin activity.

3. "El Niño"

Upwellings can be caused by changes in the upper atmosphere, such as the direction of the jet stream. Changes in the normal flow of the jet stream can cause an "El Niño," a warm current flowing north along the west coast of South America. When El Niño moves farther north than normal it changes the direction of the jet stream over Florida, which pushes ocean water against the continental shelf, causing cold water upwelling and cooler than normal surface temperatures.

During the summer, El Niño can change the normal southeasterly flow of surface winds, switching them to a northerly direction (usually northwest). Northerly winds break up weedlines and cool surface water temperatures.

The result of cool surface water run-off and northerly winds is a sudden slowdown in dolphin surface-feeding activity. Cool surface water run-off, caused by the movement of the Gulf Stream, will last only one or two days. Changes in the flow of the jet stream by El Niño moving north, resulting in cool surface water run-off and northerly winds could produce poor surface-feeding conditions for a month or more.

In later chapters I will be discussing how to use the downrigger (deep-troll) and other techniques to catch dolphin that are reluctant to surface feed during cool surface temperatures and up-welling conditions.

A Summer Without Dolphin

Dolphin are the highlight of summer sportfishing along most of the Florida coast. During my 30-plus years of blue water fishing in the Gulf Stream, this fact became even more evident one June several years ago.

The schools of dolphin normally abundant in the Gulf Stream were not to be found. I discovered after some experimentation that the dolphin were there but would not surface feed, they seemed to prefer that part of the water column some 30 feet below the surface.

We were able to catch quite a few dolphin by using the deep troll with small lures and baits. I also noted that the surface winds would switch from the normal southeast to a northerly direction around 11:00 am every day – very unusual in June. June is a month when the trade winds are normally predominantly from the southeast.

Having more questions than answers, I contacted the late Dr. Gilbert Voss at the University of Miami Rosenstiel School of Marine and Atmospheric Science. Dr. Voss, being devoted to the sea and its marine inhabitants, could not pass up an opportunity to find a possible explanation to my strange observations.

The actions of the dolphin followed the same pattern as fish avoiding cooler surface-water run-off associated with upwelling caused by Gulf Stream movements and northerly surface wind direction.

Dr. Voss alluded to one possible explanation: An El Niño had moved the atmospheric jet streams farther north and was responsible for a number of climatic changes affecting large areas. Jet streams that normally flowed west to east over the Keys during the summer were altered by El Niño and flowed east to west. These upper level easterly winds cause up-welling along the continental shelf in 600 feet of water, some 12 miles offshore, bringing cold water from the bottom to the surface. A changing surface wind direction from the normal warm southerly to a cool northerly further deteriorated surface feeding patterns by breaking up weedlines.

El Niño affects the dolphin fishery along the Atlantic and Pacific coasts and can even alter migrations as currents and isotherms change. Catching dolphin during an El Niño can be very difficult, all but eliminating anglers lacking specialized skill and techniques. A summer without dolphin in the blue water is like a summer without sunshine.

PART 3

MARINE BIRDS AND DOLPHIN

Chapter VIII
The Birds

1. "Bird Activity and Dolphin"

Marine bird activity is the single best indicator of surface-feeding activity in the ocean. I have always placed a great deal of importance on bird activity or lack of bird activity, and have learned a great deal from the action of birds in the marine environment. Marine birds must find surface-feeding fish in order to survive. Your challenge will be to find the birds and interpret their activity.

There are many species of marine birds that follow surface-feeding fish, and the species will change as fish and birds migrate through with the seasons. By identifying birds most often found during certain seasons and understanding their actions, you can differentiate between school dolphin and tuna feeding and pick out larger dolphin from smaller feeding schools. This allows you to spend time chasing big dolphin rather than small tuna or the smaller feeding schools of dolphin.

It would be easy for the inexperienced angler to assume that larger dolphin are found feeding under man-o-war birds and smaller school dolphin under the smaller terns. This, however, is not true. The size of marine birds feeding over dolphin is more properly related to the size of the prey the dolphin are feeding on than to the size of the feeding fish.

The number of smaller terns and direction of travel can tell the alert angler the size and number of the dolphin. During the fall migration, large numbers of terns feeding over dolphin moving in the same direction as the current will mean small feeding schools. Smaller numbers of terns feeding over dolphin moving into the current will mean larger, adult dolphin.

2. "Man-O-War Bird"

The man-o-war or frigate bird – a graceful flier with a wing span reaching 90 inches – is an efficient glider, soaring to great heights without moving a wing. The man-o-war prefers large flying fish and baitfish of 6 to 12 inches, but lacks the ability to land or dive into the water, so often resorts to robbing terns and gulls of their prey.

Man-o-war depend on larger gamefish such as adult dolphin, sailfish, marlin and larger tunas to drive bait to the surface or flush flying fish into the air so they can swoop down and pluck the bait-fish from the surface or catch flying fish in the air.

24. Man-O-War Bird

3. "Common, Royal and Roseate Terns"

Terns prefer smaller baitfish and often feed above the feeding schools of game-fish that force the bait up to where the terns can pluck the prey from the surface. Terns aggressively pursue small flying fish flushed out by feeding dolphin.

Terns often hover over a small piece of seaweed in a weedline and, as dolphin approach, lift the seaweed out of the water, leaving dozens of small baitfish with no protection as the dolphin attack. The terns will then drop the grass and return to pick off bait forced to the surface by the dolphin. It can be very interesting to stop fishing and just watch the interaction of the fish and birds.

4. "Smaller, Immature Terns"

These small, white terns with wing spans of 8 to 10 inches feed primarily over feeding schools of small, juvenile fish like bonito, tuna, dolphin and blue runners. Preferring small bait-fish from 1 to 2 inches in length, small terns gather over the smaller feeding schools.

Although this size schooling fish isn't the angler's target, larger gamefish often feed with or on these small feeding schools. In the case of dolphin, these small juvenile feeding schools found under small gulls in late April and May are usually accompanied by several large bulls and cows which cannibalize the smaller dolphin.

5. "Sooty Tern"

The sooty tern gets its name from its dark, sooty color. A skilled flyer with a wing span of about 20 inches, this dark tern catches surface fish in flight, darting from side to side above feeding schools of flying fish and bait driven to the surface by feeding fish. Preferring baitfish of 2 to 4 inches, they search out the feeding schools of dolphin and tuna. Sooty terns often follow adult feeding schools and large dolphin feeding on flying fish.

Due to their dark color and the dark blue water of the Gulf Stream south of the Keys, anglers will often have to remove their sunglasses to even see, at a distance, flocks of feeding sooty terns. Staying low in the boat where the dark birds can be seen contrasted against a lighter sky can work to your advantage.

Sooty terns arrive off the Keys in June, feeding over the Gulf Stream through most of the summer, gradually working south to the Dry Tortugas (a small group of islands located 70 miles west of Key West) where they breed in September.

25. Sooty Terns

6. "Noddy Tern"

Very dark-colored birds with 20-inch wing spans, noddy terns are found over the Gulf Stream in the Florida Straits most of the summer. These terns are found darting in and around small patches of sargassum seaweed, chasing small baits, and are not a good indication of feeding fish. Noddy terns are actually in competition with the dolphin. These birds prefer to catch their own bait with no help from feeding fish and their actions can confuse you and waste your time.

Noddy terns swim rapidly just below the surface, chasing bait from one seaweed clump to another, often extending the tip of a black wing above the surface and looking just like a billfish fin. I've been caught on more than one occasion, running over with a bait to throw on what I thought was a feeding sailfish, only to find a noddy tern surfacing.

Sooty, common and roseate terns will gather over feeding noddy terns, just as they will over feeding fish, diving on and catching small baitfish forced out of the seaweed by the noddy terns, although, occasionally a stray dolphin, tuna or small billfish may actually be found feeding in the area.

26. Noddy Terns

7. "Migrating Birds"

Numerous migrating birds pass off the Keys, including gannet, blue-faced booby and brown booby, but these are poor indicators of feeding fish. However, since migrating birds fly along the edges of warm currents to find baitfish, they can offer some information about the location of baitfish or currents that could help the angler.

Osprey, sparrows, blue cranes, white ibis, pelicans, ducks and crown pigeon are just a few of the other birds seen migrating across the Gulf Stream off the Keys.

Chapter IX
Identifying the Fish

1. "Identifying Fish by Bird Activity"

Dolphin caught while feeding in open blue water account for about 60 percent of the fishery, while only 20 percent are caught on flotsam and jetsam and the other 20 percent on sargassum weedlines.

In the open expanses of the Gulf Stream, the actions of feeding tuna are different from the actions of feeding dolphin, and you can easily separate the two by observing the actions of the birds over them. Birds on weedlines are a different situation entirely.

> *The action of birds over feeding tuna*
> Feeding tuna (skipjack, blackfin and small yellowfin) suddenly appear at the surface and begin feeding. Then, after a few minutes, they will sound, move a few hundred yards laterally to the direction of the current, and pop up to surface-feed again. As the tuna sound, the birds gain height above the water and break up so they can follow the movement of the school until surface feeding resumes.

During active surface-feeding, the birds will gather close to the surface of the water, darting side to side, catching baitfish. You will often see birds wind-milling as they catch baitfish, rising rapidly so that when a baitfish is dropped another bird can catch the fish before it re-enters the water.

The action of birds over feeding dolphin
In open water, feeding schools of dolphin move in a straight line, paralleling the direction of the current, remaining at the surface of the water. The birds will dart back and forth but travel in a straight line parallel to the direction of the flow of current.

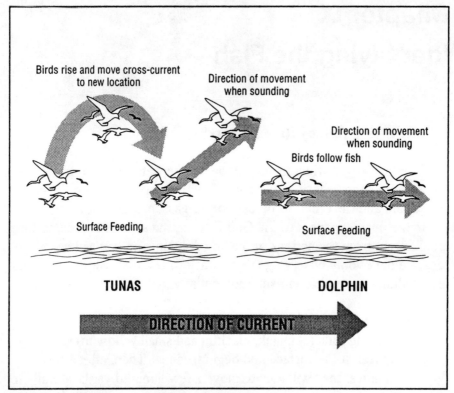

27. Birds feeding over dolphin or tuna

2. "Determining the size of dolphin"

It's possible to identify not only the species but the size of feeding game fish by the birds. Separating birds feeding over dolphin from birds feeding over tuna was the first step. Determining swimming direction of dolphin in relation to current is the next step.

Generally, during the spring and summer, larger dolphin will feed swimming *"into"* the current and smaller dolphin will feed swimming *"with"* the current.

This observation is most accurate during summer, when dolphin are not migrating, but is still fairly reliable during the spring dolphin migration when there is a strong tendency of dolphin to swim in a northerly direction. During the southerly fall migration, into the current, most of the dolphin are larger and this trend is less reliable.

In the off-migratory season, however, it's very common for juvenile dolphin feeding schools to move with the direction of the flow of current. It's also very common for adult feeding/spawning schools and mature pods of dolphin to feed in the opposite direction, into the current.

Also, larger dolphin generally have fewer birds with them. If you are faced with a situation where two groups of feeding birds are within sight, one group with many birds traveling with the current and the other with fewer birds traveling against the current, check out the group with few birds and feeding into the current. You will be glad you did.

If one of the two groups of birds is observed rising 100 feet or so above the water, then moving laterally across the current several hundred yards before feeding begins again, that's small tuna – not dolphin.

3. "Birds following dolphin feeding on weedlines"

These birds are in one of two modes: "flying and looking" or "darting and feeding." Birds flying along weedlines are excellent indicators of dolphin swimming below. Birds darting from side to side right on the surface of the water are signs of actual surface-feeding activity.

Flying and looking is a good sign that dolphin have been feeding and the birds are trying to locate them. Darting and feeding is a sign of active surface-feeding.

A weedline without birds, even after you follow it for a while, is not a good sign. If dolphin are not present it could be for a number of reasons:

Upwelling: When surface temperatures are too cool. Solution, deep troll.

PART 4

FISHING FOR DOLPHIN

CHAPTER X
Dolphin Fishing by Season

1. "Dolphin Seasons"

Here we'll go through the entire yearly cycle of dolphin feeding patterns and examine some of the angling techniques used to capture dolphin at different times.

Each month of the year brings a different set of winds, currents and dominant food sources to the marine environment. The dolphin has learned to adapt to its changing world − it's only the angler that sometimes becomes confused when confronted with the dolphin's new and different feeding patterns.

For the purpose of understanding the whole cycle, the dolphin year can be broken into four seasons: "winter" (December, January and February), "spring" (March, April and May), "summer" (June, July and August) and "fall" (September, October and November).

These seasons describe changes in dolphin activity that occur with temperature and salinity changes, and will vary slightly from year to year. Variations will occur when the weather warms early in the winter or cools early at the end of summer.

As we move through the four seasons of dolphin activity in the Florida Straits, south of the Lower Keys and Key West, you will note that one season begins to blend into the next. The cycle of seasons usually remains constant, but moves forward or backward on your calendar reflecting the early or late temperature changes.

It's also important to note that these dolphin seasons reflect the activity of dolphin in the Florida Straits and will occur later or earlier in other areas as the dolphin migrate northward or southward during the course of the season, following the isotherms.

2. "The Winter Season (December, January and February)"

Dolphin follow isotherms (areas of preferred water temperature) south as winter begins, narrowing their distribution to the equatorial zone – a narrow band extending about 20° to the north and south of the equator. This zone enjoys excellent year-round dolphin fishing under favorable conditions.

During the winter season off the lower Florida coast and Key West, dolphin fishing can be very productive on the warm southerly winds that develop between cold fronts passing through the Florida Straits. At this time, target dolphin on the second day of favorable southerly winds, giving surface conditions in the Gulf Stream and the dolphin time to adjust.

A variety of sizes of dolphin are found in the Straits during the winter season, including adult feeding schools, spawning schools, and pods of large bulls and cows. The southerly winds begin to push the clear cobalt-blue flow of Gulf Stream water against the murky blue-green inshore water driven offshore by the north winds of preceding cold fronts. The blue-green water will usually be a counter current and develop a rip, drawing flotsam and jetsam along its edge.

This action develops an offshore color change and rip that is perfect for dolphin feeding activity. The dolphin will continue to feed along the color change until the next cold front moves through, shifting the wind to the north.

Trolling baits along the color change works extremely well with the bait and fish concentrated. Trolling in the blue water beyond the color change requires the use of artificial lures or bait/lure combinations so that larger areas can be covered with the greater trolling speeds offered by artificial baits.

February is a transition month in the winter season. In February, large female dolphin in the off-spawning cycle begin to spin inshore from the Gulf Stream searching for coastal tide lines which occur in 180 to 400 feet of water. Sailfish, kingfish, tuna and wahoo provide most of the blue water action during the winter season in these depths and the arrival of the dolphin makes a nice addition to the sportfishing.

Ballyhoo are the most commonly used bait in this fishery and the dolphin will respond with gusto. Baits are generally preferred to lures in this fishery because coastal tide rips are close to shore and the fish are in a concentrated area.

Winds in the northerly quadrant are common this time of year as cold fronts move across Florida and through the Straits. The wind, one of the most important factors in dolphin fishing generally makes a complete cycle this time of year, every three to five days. Southerly winds remain for a day or so after a front passes then begin shifting to the west and northwest as a new front approaches. As the front passes overhead brisk northerly winds follow, gradually shifting to the northeast and east behind the front.

Fishing cycles with the wind direction this time of the year. Sailfish, tuna and wahoo bite best during the northerly winds and the dolphin become aggressive with the easterly and southerly winds behind the front. Dolphin catches will be greatly diminished on the north winds but there are techniques to catch dolphin even with a north wind (See: *"Dolphin on Deep Troll"* Chapter XIII-4).

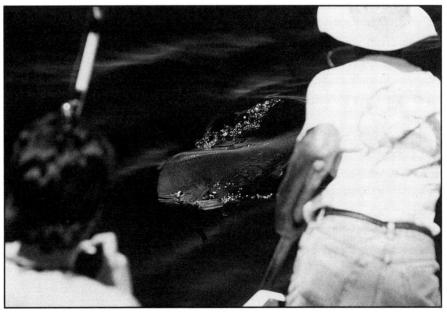

28. A Bull Dolphin is led to the gaff.

3. "The Spring Season (March, April and May)"

This is a season of transition for dolphin and many other pelagic gamefish that migrate north as the water gradually warms. During the winter season the dolphin were held close to the equator by cold water pushing south with the cold fronts. Now that the days are growing longer and warmer, the cold water begins to warm, sending a signal to dolphin that it's time to migrate north. The dolphin instinctively begin to follow the isotherms as they move away from the equator.

Along the Florida Keys, dolphin action increases each day in March with flurries of activity during warm spells between cold fronts. In the last week of March, cold fronts begin to stall and increasing days of warm southerly winds warm the water.

During April, dolphin are abundant in the Florida Straits south of the Keys, moving north on the warm southerly winds, then moving south, tailing on the surface with the cool northerly winds that accompany persistent cold fronts.

At this time, schools of dolphin are particularly abundant in 300 to 500 feet of water, traveling in a narrow corridor of current passing close to the Keys, some 7 to 12 miles offshore.

Fishing techniques for dolphin differ at this time of the year depending on whether the fish are tailing or migrating. Fishing migrating dolphin on a southerly wind is easy. They are aggressive and trolled baits or artificials work well. Dolphin can be located by trolling in the 300 to 500 foot depth and watching for turtles, boards or feeding birds.

Quite often, a single dolphin will give away the location of the school by jumping from the water, turning on its side and splashing into the water. This form of school behavior sends out an audible sound so other dolphin can locate the school.

Fishing for tailing dolphin is more difficult. Tailing occurs when current opposes the wind. For example: An east wind and an eastbound current. These fish have lock-jaw to conventional fishing techniques. Trolling artificials fast to run the fish down and casting live or dead ballyhoo with spinning rods right on their nose is the only method I have found to get these dolphin to feed. These are generally larger dolphin (20 to 30 pounds) moving rapidly into the current in pods of three to six fish, feeding on flying fish at the surface. Man-o-war birds often follow these pods to pick off the flying fish as they are forced into the air (See: *"Techniques for fishing tailing dolphin"* Chapter XIII-3).

By May, cold fronts are history and the dolphin are swimming steadily north following the isotherms. This is the ideal time to fish for dolphin. The weather is calm and the fish will eat almost anything. At this time, remember that the dolphin want to swim north, so don't try to troll south. Always troll north with spring migrations, this will hold the interest of the dolphin longer.

Schools encountered in May are primarily feeding schools accompanied by several large adult bulls and cows. Because of the narrow corridor of migration, trolled ballyhoo work well. Care should be used to size the baits carefully (See: *"Sizing Baits"* Chapter XII-1).

Catching small dolphin, although not always the angler's target, is still necessary in order to attract and catch the larger dolphin.

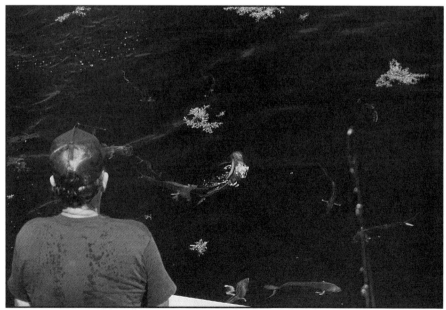

29. School of dolphin (feeding school)

4. "Summer Season (June, July and August)"

In June, the trade winds begin to blow across the Gulf Stream from the southeast, averaging 12 to 18 miles per hour, and the dolphin spread south offshore into the Gulf Stream. The best dolphin fishing in June is usually 12 to 18 miles offshore in 600 to 800 feet of water.

However, at this time of the year, the dolphin move around, seeking the greatest abundance of food. Weedlines develop more commonly in late June and increasing in July and August as the sargassum continues to grow.

Overall, fewer than 20 percent of dolphin are caught on weedlines. The conditions must be right for weedline development, out-going tide, southeasterly wind and strong Gulf Stream current combine to line up pads of sargassum (See: *"Weedlines"* Chapter VI-8).

Once a weedline develops, it must be in the right depth for the time of year and it must hold bait for the dolphin. Early June can be tricky because the dolphin are feeding into the flow of the Gulf Stream on flying fish in open blue water or schooling and feeding around boards or other floating objects that hold small jacks, file fish etc. in the absence of weedline development.

In July, dolphin continue to feed in the open water under birds and concentrate under floating debris and weedlines when they develop and the bait is abundant.

August is another transition month for dolphin and many other pelagic species. The ocean water is steadily cooling as the days get shorter and the sun moves father south. Off George's Bank, Nova Scotia the dolphin have already begun to migrate south with the isotherms.

In August along Florida and the Keys, dolphin remain offshore in 600 to 800 feet of water, following the warm flow of the Gulf Stream south, occasionally coming inshore when bait is abundant. Realizing that winter is coming, the dolphin begin to swim more persistently south into the warm current, following the isotherms south toward the Equator.

By mid-August the schools traveling south along weedlines, usually in 800 feet of water, will pause to strike baits but while you are fighting the hooked fish the remainder of the school continues to move south. By the time the hooked fish are landed the school will be several hundred feet ahead.

5. "Fall Season (September, October and November)"

Migrating schools which traveled far to the north during the summer – some possibly as far as George's Bank, Nova Scotia – and began their trip south toward the equator in mid- to late summer, continue to pass off the Keys early in the fall season.

Excellent dolphin fishing can be found along the Keys in this season when winds shift to the southeast and the Gulf Stream looks like summer with dolphin schools everywhere.

I call this an "opportunity fishery" because a cold front with north winds can end dolphin fishing as quickly as it began. Early winter months concentrate baitfish close to the reef and it's not unusual to find schools of dolphin in 250 to 350 feet of water just outside the reef.

In November, 12- to 20-pound dolphin will feed close to the reef, sometimes venturing right up on the first reef in 20 feet of water. This is a time when we look for sailfish feeding on the shallow reef close to steep drop offs, showering the ballyhoo (ballyhoo jumping to escape sailfish and dolphin).

Dolphin are often seen and caught feeding on the ballyhoo with the sailfish. This is a case where having live bait (ballyhoo, threadfin herring or pilchards) is a must. Dolphin or sailfish feeding on schools of ballyhoo will not look at any other bait.

To catch dolphin and sailfish feeding on top of the reef, live baits on spinning tackle are sight-cast directly to the fish as they are feeding.

30. Ballyhoo, common baitfish

Chapter XI
Fishing Techniques By Month

1. "East Winds of April"

In April, dolphin begin their northerly migration as the water warms. Key West is on the northern limits of the dolphin's winter home and any time during the winter when the wind shifts to the south dolphin begin to appear. Along the Florida Keys this northward migration actually moves east due to east-west orientation of the islands. In some years we catch dolphin right through the winter months.

Easterly winds behind cold fronts struggling to push their way into the Florida Straits in late winter can reach a rather brisk 18 to 20 knots. Seas of 3 to 5 feet are normal and the east-bound current along the Keys presents "tailing conditions" for dolphin. Using the upper cyclonic energy of the waves stacked up by the opposing current, the dolphin tend to surface-feed on flying fish, the most abundant food source this time of year.

The Florida Current, a narrow belt of current running inshore of the mighty Gulf Stream, flows close to shore at this time of the year. The shoreward edge of the Florida Current is in 300 feet of water and the offshore edge in 500 feet. Larger bull and cow dolphin, ranging from 15 to 30 pounds, spin off the northerly flow of the Gulf Stream, approximately 20 miles offshore, and feed in the Florida Current closer to shore.

The man-o-war or frigate bird, which depends on dolphin and other surface-feeding game fish to force baitfish to the surface, becomes the angler's best tool this time of year.

The April stage is now set: Dolphin tailing in 300 to 500 feet of water, feeding on flying fish, and man-o-war birds circling overhead, ready to catch the flying fish as they are forced into the air.

Dolphin: The Perfect Gamefish

TECHNIQUE

It's a little difficult to get April dolphin to eat a bait or artificial. They're feeding on nice, fresh flying fish that present a challenge to catch. The wind is cool, generally from the east-northeast or east, making the dolphin reluctant to be aggressive.

Don't be disappointed if several big dolphin run right through your baits chasing flying fish and pay no attention to you or the baits. As the 11 a.m. to 1 p.m. hours approach, these fish will become more aggressive on the baits. That's because dolphin will feed with a number of other oceanic game fish, including sailfish, wahoo and blackfin tuna, but avoid feeding with other species such as skipjack tuna or bonito.

Since skipjack, among the most abundant fish in the ocean, feed from daylight to around 11 a.m. and then dive into the depths to avoid warming surface water, dolphin wait until the skipjack dive before feeding aggressively at the surface.

31. Angler with a skip jack tuna.

The angler and captain must work together, find the man-o-war birds, locate the dolphin surfing down the seas, and launch a coordinated attack on the tailing fish. Baits or artificial lures can be used. I prefer artificials, which allow the angler the flexibility to run the fish down under the birds. Baits work well, but using speed to catch the birds will destroy the baits by the time you get there.

If you elect to use artificials you must also have a 20-pound class spinning rod handy with a castable ballyhoo rig (See: *"Sight Casting To Dolphin"* Chapter XIII-1) ready to throw in case they don't take the artificials. Often 20- to 30-pound dolphin will come running in, but will hesitate to take the artificials, particularly when the wind is east/northeast. Then you must try to set off the dolphin's "flying fish reflex." Baits splashing down near feeding dolphin will get instant attention from dolphin, accustomed to attacking flying fish during the split second it takes them to land and take off again.

Once the first dolphin is hooked, shift to the open window technique.

OPEN WINDOW TECHNIQUE

This technique is designed for larger dolphin and works best in the spring season (March and April). Once a dolphin is hooked there is a short period of time when other large dolphin will take a bait. I call this the "open window." As long as a hooked fish is in the water, other large fish will feed. Once the hooked fish is removed from the water this window of opportunity closes and the dolphin will no longer feed.

To take advantage of this opportunity, hold the hooked fish 30 feet behind the boat and drop another bait (a ballyhoo rig on castable spin or trolling gear) behind the hooked fish. Other large dolphin will remain aggressive feeders and take the bait. Boat the first fish and fight the second to about 30 feet astern and drop the third bait behind the hooked fish for another hook-up. Sometimes five or six 20- to 30-pound dolphin can be caught using this method.

2. "Light East Winds of May"

In lighter east winds of 10 to 15 mph, dolphin stop tailing and return to their pelagic migratory mission. In April and May, dolphin have a strong desire to swim toward the northeast off the lower Keys and, during lighter winds, often swim on the surface.

In light winds, dolphin can be located by watching for individuals jumping in slow arches, landing on their sides as they re-enter the water. This is school behavior and different fish alternate jumping.

Migrating turtles attract schools of small minnows, and dolphin often adopt one of these large sea turtles. No turtle should be overlooked at this time of year.

Dolphin: The Perfect Gamefish

When you spot dolphin, troll around the area and be prepared to go into a cut-bait and light-spinner mode of fishing (See: *"Chumming"* Chapter XIII-2). When the first dolphin is hooked, hold the fish in the water and, using light spinners and cut bait, hook additional fish. One fish (average size is 4 to 6 pounds) must remain in the water to keep the school near, and it's a good idea to keep a fresh-hooked fish in the water, since fresh-hooked fish help you chum by regurgitating minnows.

Because of their migratory mission, school fish may swim away if you stop the boat, even if you have additional fish hooked. Idling to the north (or east in the lower Keys) with the migrations will help keep the fish with you. If you lose the school, look east/north of your location.

Be ready for larger, 15- to 30-pound fish that accompany these school fish, often feeding on the smaller dolphin. A large, rigged ballyhoo will allow you to get the bait past the school fish and hook up the larger dolphin. You may have to use a live, small, school dolphin for bait if the larger fish are feeding on the schoolies.

32. Mating turtles attract dolphin schools

TECHNIQUE

This time of year, dolphin are in 300 to 500 feet of water. Trolling in lighter winds is not too demanding. The dolphin are generally small and respond to trolled baits or artificials very quickly. I recommend trolling with small, rigged ballyhoo or an assortment of small artificials until you locate a school of dolphin around a turtle or under birds. Pull baits past each turtle. It's important to stay far enough away to attract a strike but not close enough to scare the turtle down. If a turtle dives the dolphin may go down with it.

There are plenty of big dolphin with the schools of smaller fish, but this time of year you need to make some noise and create some excitement by hooking and catching the school dolphin. During the confusion, big dolphin will get excited and come running in to feed with or on the small dolphin, then you can hook up the bigger dolphin using larger baits or live small dolphin.

If a big bull comes in and is reluctant to eat a bait, use a large ballyhoo or flying fish rigged with a mono leader on a spinning rod and cast it close to the dolphin, allowing it to splash down on the surface. When the dolphin runs over, give it a couple of erratic jerks and get ready to set the hook. Once one large dolphin is hooked, maneuver the boat and go to the open window technique, feeding other baits back behind the hooked fish.

Trolled ballyhoo work well this time of year because there is less area to cover. Keep baits small because dolphin have a great awareness of bait size (See: *"Bait Size"* Chapter XII-1).

If you fish near a populated area such as Miami, artificials might have an advantage. You can move around quickly and find the fish before the rest of the fleet arrive.

Weedlines sometimes do form this time of year but generally they come in June. Boards and other flotsam in the 300-500 foot depth will most likely be loaded with dolphin provided positive conditions for dolphin surface feeding activity exist. Perhaps the single most important thing to remember in May is that there are a lot of dolphin migrating in this depth, but often you must create some excitement to draw in the bigger fish.

Engage school dolphin even if you have caught your personal limit – the fish can be released. This action will draw in the 20- and 30-pound fish. Using the open window technique and bigger baits you can isolate the larger dolphin.

3. "Southeasterly Trade Winds of June"

In June, southeasterly trade winds develop along the Florida Keys, maintaining speeds of 14 to 18 mph. The axis of the Gulf Stream, located in 600 to 800 feet of water, becomes the predominant current flow, overshadowing the Florida Current as it slows down at this time of the year. Dolphin instinctively move offshore some 12 to 15 miles to find the sargassum weedlines that begin to build as the surface-growing, brownish-yellow/green algae matures and floats northward with the Gulf Stream.

The opposing forces of Gulf Stream flow, inshore tides and southeasterly trade winds form surface-fishing conditions that make experienced captains' hearts beat fast in the anticipation of dolphin action along weedlines and rips that bring giant dolphin and school fish together in a bonanza of dolphin fishing action.

TECHNIQUE

In June on a southeasterly wind, the best depth will generally be 600 to 800 feet. Dolphin will feed on weedlines provided there are positive factors for development (See: *"WeedLines"* Chapter VI-8).

Now is the time to use artificial lures. Dolphin fishing in June requires the angler to cover great distances to locate forming weedlines and fish working under birds. Once dolphin are located, the Angler can choose between trolled baits and artificials.

Weedlines: Weedlines present the single best surface structure for attracting dolphin. They concentrate bait and offer boards and other flotsam for dolphin to form schools around. Trolling alongside the weedlines is the best method of fishing them. If weedlines are not developed, or if the most abundant source of bait is in open blue water, then the dolphin will be feeding under birds (See: *"Birds"* Chapter VIII).

Many anglers run straight offshore to find the weedlines this time of year. It's not a bad idea to run to the 600- to 800- foot depth, but one must realize that weedlines are not always one continuous line. Often, numerous short weedlines ½ to 2 miles long parallel the flow of the current. One large, continuous line can easily be located by just running offshore but the broken lines must be found by trolling and covering lots of area.

Artificials or baits can be sized up to catch only the larger dolphin. Artificials will work best when there are a lot of dolphin; they require less time to unhook a fish and no time making up baits. This is important when school dolphin are so plentiful you can't even get a bait out.

Large tuna, wahoo or marlin may strike lures trolled along weedlines and with this in mind you might want to have Penn International 30-Wide out just in case. If you prefer lighter-tackle action, stop alongside the weedline when you encounter a school and use spinning tackle and cut bait to catch the schoolies.

Flotsam: Fishing dolphin around boards or floating debris is also easy. For one thing, the flotsam will hold the school, provided the angler takes care not to pull the school too far away from the floating object. Once you confirm the flotsam is holding dolphin, a variety of techniques can be used depending on the size and number of fish. Keeping the boat within 100 feet of floating objects will reduce the possibility of losing the school. A marker buoy can be used to mark the flotsam, making returning to the location easier (See: Appendix H, *"How to make a marker buoy"*). Remember, on a north wind the deep-troll can be used with great success when conventional methods fail (See: *"Deep-Troll"* Chapter XIII-4).

33. Dolphin feeding around patches of sargassum seaweed

Open Blue Water: Dolphin feeding in open blue water are more difficult to catch. First the angler has to find the fish and attract a strike. After a dolphin is hooked the school must be kept near the boat by keeping a hooked fish in the water while other members of the school are caught.

Finding the dolphin in open blue water is easy if you pay close attention to bird activity (See: *"Birds"* Chapter VIII). Use fast-troll and artificial lures to run the dolphin down and then switch to the open window technique (See: Chapter XI), flying fish reflex (See: *"Flying Fish Reflex"* Chapter XIII-1) or bait and chunk (See:*Chumming* Chapter XIII-2) to catch additional fish.

4. "Mid-Summer"

In mid-summer, dolphin tend to be more domestic, hanging out under boards and weedlines or chasing bait in the open expanses of the Gulf Stream. The dolphin's strong migratory tendency to move northward as the water warms in spring and to move south as winter begins are relaxed during the summer months.

TECHNIQUE

This time of year, trolling along weedlines with ballyhoo or casting small pieces of cut bait with light spinning tackle while drifting can be the experience of a lifetime. At times there are so many dolphin around weedlines that catching fish is not a problem. The problem is getting the smaller school dolphin to let your baits alone long enough to catch the larger dolphin. Often you can't get a bait past the school fish even when you can see the 30-pound bulls right behind the boat.

5. "South Winds of Late July and Early August"

In late July and August, the wind along the Keys comes predominantly from the south. It is a soft wind with calm seas and crystal clear water. The abundant sargassum seaweed floating in the Gulf Stream continues to grow through the summer and large patches continue to build with positive conditions. By late summer, patches of seaweed can measure more than 100 feet in diameter.

Floating northward in the Gulf Stream, these sargassum patches are generally found outside of 800 feet of water, some 15 to 18 miles offshore. They support schools of small blue runners and other baitfish which in turn attract large numbers of gamefish including dolphin, wahoo and billfish.

TECHNIQUE

Fishing these patches is essentially like fishing a weedline. The patches usually float several hundred feet apart and may run for long distances, paralleling the flow of the current along the Keys and drifting slowly inshore with the southerly wind.

Trolling baits near the patches will provoke strikes from hungry dolphin. Late in the summer large numbers of school-size dolphin, averaging from 6 to 10 pounds with plenty of 12- to 16-pound fish mixed in, will be first to strike. Roaming bands of larger bulls and cows will join into the action as it progresses. These are adult mating schools, compared to the juvenile feeding schools of May when the average schoolie weighed 4 to 6 pounds.

Fishing sargassum patches is easy. Once schools of dolphin are encountered the captain should try to keep the boat close to the patch. The patches are large and easily relocated after fighting a fish. When dolphin are scared by passing predators, or just get bored with you, they will return to the patch. Dolphin that are drawn too far away from patches, however, may just swim away into the blue water. This is true with boards and other flotsam as well.

Anglers should expect to run offshore until they find surface conditions that attract baitfish and dolphin. Most captains will run out to 600 feet of water and fast-troll with artificials.

Trolling into the 800-foot depth, a selection of different size artificial lures should be used to attract strikes from the school dolphin as well as the larger bulls and cows. Remember that, although the 5-pound dolphin is not the target size, the resulting surface excitement will attract other fish and 40-pound bulls and cows will run up and try to eat a school dolphin after it is hooked.

Once a dolphin is hooked, particularly if it is a larger fish, you must slow the boat to fight the fish. Now is the time to take the other artificials out of the water and slip the trolling baits behind the hooked fish for more hook-ups.

Tackle should be selected carefully. Once you have encountered plenty of dolphin action, the secret is to scale up the size of the baits or lures to attract only the larger fish. If the dolphin appear to slow down, be sure to keep at least one small bait or lure out to attract strikes from the school dolphin which will again draw the larger fish into the action.

Additional dolphin traveling with the hooked fish will take baits as long as the first hooked fish is left in the water. Once the first fish is removed, secondary hook-ups are much harder.

6. "Late August and September"

In late August and September, the warm southerly winds of summer begin to hint of winter. As nights grow cooler and days get shorter, dolphin once again show signs of a strong desire to migrate. This time the dolphin move south (or west off the lower Keys and Key West).

Oddly, the dolphin now stay offshore in 640 to 2,000 feet of water (12 to 20 miles from shore). Apparently dolphin rely on the northward flow of the Gulf Stream current to navigate, sensing direction from the current and utilizing the abundant food found around the sargassum seaweed.

Fishing for these migrating fish, the angler must reverse the thinking of April, when the fish wanted to continue north, and prepare to troll and move in a southerly (or west in Lower Keys and Key West) direction with the flow of the migration.

At this time of year, migrating dolphin will run off and leave the boat while you are fighting fish. The captain will have to troll rapidly in the direction of migration to catch the school.

Late in September the seaweed takes on the look of logs, rolled into large, rounded, floats by the interaction of more frequent northerly winds and strong Gulf Stream current.

Dolphin in September become more tolerant of the northerly winds, frequently surface-feeding, particularly in the morning before the large high-pressure areas to the north build with the warming day, producing stronger, northerly winds in the afternoon. Light northerly winds in the morning often increase by noon and by afternoon can exceed 20 knots.

TECHNIQUE

Fast-moving schools of migrating dolphin can be fished with bait or artificial lures. I like the artificial lures, the captain can run the fish down and not worry about tearing up the bait. Rigged baits should be kept ready. After the hook-up using artificial bait, rigged ballyhoo can be dropped back or cast to capitalize on the open-window.

A 20-pound, castable spinning outfit is used for casting to dolphin, or a 20/30-pound-test rotary spoon outfit with a rigged trolling ballyhoo can be dropped back into the fishing area.

While fighting a fish at reduced speeds, artificial lures become ineffective and baits must be used.

7. "Northeast Winds of October, November and December"

Dolphin, abundant off South Florida and the Keys during the summer, become only an occasional catch in October and November (allowing for some seasonal variations). Most of the large migrations have already pushed south into the Florida Straits.

Food sources in the blue water become scarce and sailfish, tuna and dolphin will feed right on top of the shallow reef. Off the Keys, when conditions are right, roaming bands of large dolphin weighing 16 to 30 pounds can show up right on top of the reef in 20 feet of water. For many years, charter captains have watched the shallow reef close to sheer drops from 20 to 90 feet for sprays of ballyhoo that signal feeding bands of sailfish and occasionally dolphin and tuna.

The conditions that bring this unusual fishery to the shallow reef are these: A Gulf Stream meander brings the deep blue water very close to the reef. Northeast winds of winter bring the large schools of ballyhoo close to the edge of the drop and predators – barracuda and mackerel – drive them into the blue water over the edge of the reef.

Dolphin traveling in groups of 20 to 50 large adult fish begin to feed on the ballyhoo, driving them back into the 20-foot reef. Alert anglers observing the stomach contents of the dolphin will find houndfish (similar to needle fish) and ballyhoo in dolphin stomachs when this phenomenon is taking place. Indications of feeding dolphin on the reef are man-o-war birds or ballyhoo sprays on the shallow reef (See: *"Birds"* Chapter VIII).

TECHNIQUE

With the northeast wind and cooler water, dolphin are hard to get to bite – but the sheer size and sport of the event compels the angler to action. Live bait is a must in getting these dolphin to strike. Occasionally, well-made fresh baits will attract strikes but live bait is a sure thing.

Chum up the ballyhoo on the reef and, with a cast net or small hair hooks, catch three or four dozen ballyhoo. Watch for the ballyhoo showers along the sheer drop of the reef, in 20 to 90 feet of water, and move in quickly, casting with large spinners and live ballyhoo to the feeding dolphin.

Once a dolphin is hooked, shift to the open window technique, keeping one fish hooked to hold the school, and bait with fresh, dead ballyhoo. If possible, pull the school to the deep side of the reef, avoiding barracuda on top of the reef.

Large-capacity spinning reels with 300 yards of 20-pound-test monofilament line work best. This occasional phenomenon requires the right conditions, but when it happens it's worth being there and knowing what to do.

Chapter XII

Baits vs. Lures

1. "Sizing Baits and Lures"

After more than 30 years of examining the stomach contents of dolphin and reviewing the findings of scientists from around the world, I can tell you that dolphin have a very size-conscious diet. Dolphin generally prefer baitfish ranging from 1 to 6 inches in length, depending on their size.

The overwhelming majority of baitfish found in the stomachs of dolphin feeding on weedlines are 1 to 4 inches in length. Flying fish from 4 to 6 inches are commonly found in stomachs of adult dolphin feeding in open blue water. Some notable exceptions occur when large dolphin (20 pounds and over) occasionally cannibalize 3- to 5-pound school dolphin.

Some of the more unusual items I have found in dolphin stomachs over the years include a plastic cigarette lighter, white ibis bird, tar balls and sea horses. At certain times of the year, small yellow sea horses (1 to 3 inches in length) are abundant in the sargassum seaweed of the Gulf Stream. In both dolphin and tuna stomachs I often find sea horses and seaweed together– a sort of "sargassum-a-la-sea horse" salad.

Trolling smaller ballyhoo (number 16 ballyhoo, 8 inches long), one of the most commonly used dolphin baits, attracts strikes from a wide size-range of dolphin. Larger ballyhoo such as number 12, horse ballyhoo or ballyhoo/lure combinations will limit strikes to only large dolphin.

Trolling artificial lures with no bait offers the angler a much more precise method of controlling the size of the dolphin caught. Small dolphin can rip baits into smaller pieces, resulting in hook-ups, whereas lures remain constant in size and larger lures discourage strikes from smaller fish.

Controlling the size of lures and baits will control the size of dolphin caught.

Dolphin: The Perfect Gamefish

This is a very important point because during certain seasons you want to use small lures to hook small school dolphin and draw the bigger adult fish into the excitement. In other seasons when small school fish with their more aggressive nature are mixed in with larger school dolphin, you want to scale up lure size to screen out small dolphin and catch only the larger fish.

For example, a small Soft Head® lure, 4 inches in length with a diameter of ¼-inch, will attract strikes from 4- to 6-pound dolphin. Scaling up the lure size to 6-inches in length and ½-inch diameter will screen out strikes from 4- to 6-pound fish and only attract strikes from dolphin 8 to 12 pounds or larger. This simple change in lure size will improve the quality of your catch.

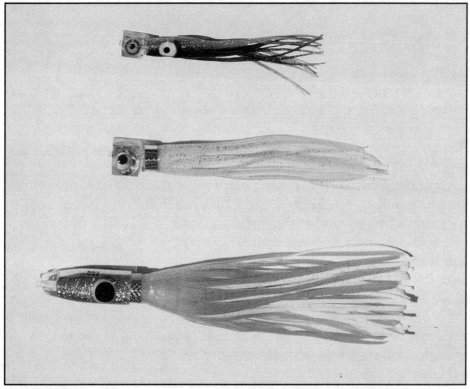

34. Increasing lure size to screen out smaller dolphin.

2. "Trolling Baits"

There are some conditions where baits work better than lures. For example: A weedline or color change with lots of larger dolphin and only a few small fish.

For baits to be successful, fish must be concentrated in an area. Maximum trolling speeds with baits is 4.5 to 5.5 knots. Adding lures in front of baits can increase speed but limit dolphin size to only larger fish.

A raging bull dolphin

Leaping cow dolphin

Dolphin greyhounding thru the air

Mate Matt McLean and a junior angler with a thirty pound dolphin

Angler displays a trophy dolphin with vertical bands of excitement

A dolphin poses for a photograph

A thirty foot long whale shark, weighing over ten tons, glides past the Sea Boots

Capt. Jim Sharpe, Jr. fights a big dolphin on fly from the Sea Boots

The most common bait for trolling is the ballyhoo. Flying fish can be used but are difficult to rig and troll. I prefer number 16 ballyhoo. Their size allows for strikes from a wide size-range of dolphin. If numerous small dolphin become a problem I would switch to artificials and size up the lures.

We use a pin rig with a single # 3407, 8/0 Mustad ring-eye hook and copper wire to attach the bait to the pin (See: Appendix B-1, *"Single Hook Ballyhoo Rig"*). Some boats use a small rubber band in place of the copper wire, but we have noticed billfish knock the bait off the pin with rubber bands but not with wire.

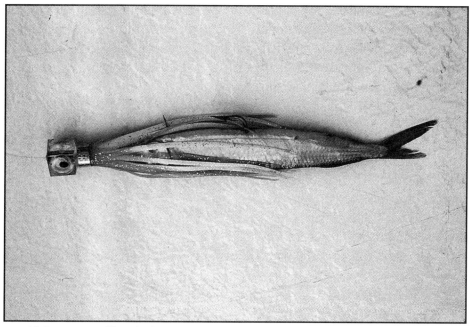

35. Sizing up trolling baits by adding a lure.

Bait Trolling Pattern

I prefer to troll four lines when trolling baits: Two long riggers, a deep-troll with double-hook mono trolling rig down 50 feet and a flat line. In the boat, ready for use, are two spinning outfits rigged with castable ballyhoo rigs on a Penn 80W and a 130-pound rod and a marlin/shark leader in reserve.

The rigger lines are set at different lengths so they don't tangle on turns, 250 feet on the long rigger and 150 feet on the short rigger. The length of the deep troll is set where it will pop up near the short rigger after being tripped by a strike. The flat line is set 75 feet astern, just behind the white water.

The double-hook mono rig on the deep troll consists of two Mustad #3407 ring-eye hooks. One hook is passed through the eye of the other to make double hooks and the ballyhoo is secured with a pin and wrapped with copper wire (See: *"Appendices B-1 & 2"*).

The double-hook rig is used to minimize cut-offs from wahoo often found under boards and along weedlines and still attract dolphin or billfish. A metal-head feather can be added in front of the double-hook rig to attract more wahoo.

3. "Trolling Artificial Lures"

A situation where lures work better than baits would be finding fast moving dolphin feeding on flying fish in open blue water. There are no speed limits with lures. When searching the Gulf Stream for dolphin, the ability to cover large areas or chase down fast-moving fish and sight-cast baits can mean success or failure. Plus, adjusting the size of the artificial lures is one of the best ways to screen out smaller fish, so the angler can choose the size dolphin he wants to catch.

Selecting lures

Lures should be selected according to size, action and their ability to avoid catching sea-weed. The flat lines should have small 4-inch lures to attract all sizes of dolphin. The outriggers should have 6-inch lures to attract larger dolphin, yellowfin tuna, white or blue marlin. I like to run a marlin lure (a 10-inch Soft Head or Sevenstrand lure) in the center just behind the flat lines to act as a teaser for big dolphin and to attract a marlin's attention. Any time you are fishing for dolphin you could attract a marlin.

Selecting and rigging tackle

On the flatlines with 4-inch lures, I recommend a Penn International 20-T reel on a Penn International ll, 20-pound rod. On the outriggers with 6-inch lures I recommend Penn International 30-T reels with Penn International ll 30-pound rods. These high-quality offshore Penn Reels have a large line capacity; the 20-T holds 720 yards of 20-pound-test line. The 30-T holds 730 yards of 30-pound line.

The center-rigger lure, rigged on a 50W Penn International reel and rod, acts as a marlin lure and big dolphin teaser. When a 400-pound blue marlin eats your dolphin lure you will be glad you invested the extra money for quality.

Lure trolling pattern

The trolling pattern for artificials is very similar to trolling baits. Each lure is set at a different distance from the boat to prevent tangling. The deep troll should be eliminated and a second flat line used in its place while fast trolling and searching for dolphin.

If you plan to use the sight-cast method, I recommend trolling only three lures, 100 feet astern – two of these on outriggers and one elevated on a center rigger so that baits can be sight-cast from either side of the stern of the boat. If the center line can't be elevated, use just the two outriggers and a flat teaser line 20 feet off the stern (See: *"Appendix G-2"*).

4. "When to Switch from Lures to Baits"

For best results, most artificials should be trolled at 5 to 7 knots. Slower speeds kill the action that makes artificials work. While fighting hooked fish at slower speeds, anglers must switch to trolled baits or sight-cast methods to attract other strikes.

Trolling leaders should be equipped with wind-on leaders and snap swivels to facilitate a quick switch to trolled baits. The snap swivel is located 8 feet above the lure in the wind-on leader so that a bait and leader can be quickly substituted for the trolling rig in the "open-window" opportunity. (See: *"Appendices A, B and C* for rigging the wind-on leader, trolling baits and artificial lures"). A small, live dolphin on a live-bait leader can be snapped on the 50- or 80-pound tackle quickly in the event a blue marlin crashes your school of dolphin (See: *"Appendix A-4"*).

Chapter XIII
Special Fishing Techniques

1. "Sight-Casting to Dolphin: Initiating the Flying fish Reflex"

What is the flying fish reflex? Many years ago, as we drifted with the current catching school dolphin, I had a 40-pound bull dolphin swimming around my boat that refused to eat anything. I tried every trick I knew to get this fish to strike, but nothing worked. In desperation I hooked a #7 live-bait hook through the nose of a fresh flying fish that had jumped into the boat earlier that day and cast the bait with a spinner several feet in front of the dolphin, making it splash several times. That big dolphin ate that bait so fast I didn't have time to close the bail.

I believe that when a flying fish takes flight and lands back in the water there is a brief second of compromise. The flying fish can't out-swim the dolphin, but it must gain speed before it can get into the air again. This is an easy time for a dolphin to catch the flying fish, if it acts quickly. The sound of a flying fish smacking the water may trigger a feeding response, similar to the ringing of Pavlov's bell, which I call the flying fish reflex.

In this technique, a rigged dead bait (ballyhoo or flying fish) or live bait rigged on a spinning rod and reel is sight-cast several feet in front of a dolphin. The captain spots the dolphin from the flying bridge or tuna tower and points it out to the angler. When the angler spots the fish he makes a low profile cast 6 to 8 feet in front of the fish.

As the bait strikes the water it skips across the surface several times. The angler stops the line and pulls the bait back toward the boat to make the bait change direction, skipping several times in the opposite direction. This action imitates a flying fish that just landed.

The bait is then allowed to sink away as the dolphin approaches. If more interest is needed, the bait can be jigged away to create a hurt-fish image. This technique generally triggers the flying fish reflex in the dolphin and generates a strike.

Trolling patterns can be modified to fit the sight-casting technique. In April, for instance, pods of 20- to 30-pound adult dolphin move rapidly west along the Keys, chasing flying fish. One of the best methods of catching these large dolphin is the sight-cast method.

We set up a pattern of 6-inch dolphin lures on two short riggers at 150 feet and a single flat line from the center of the boat. The dolphin are chased down and the lures pulled directly in front of the fish. Most of the time the dolphin are attracted, but will not strike the lures (See: Appendix G-2, *"Sight-Cast Trolling Pattern"*). This behavior is similar to that of tailing fish and a castable bait on a spinning rod-and-reel must be sight-cast right on top of the fish. These large adult fish will then turn and eat the bait, reacting to the flying fish reflex.

During the summer season, big dolphin often chase flying fish or just swim along a weedline and only react to sight-cast baits. (See: Appendix A-3, *"Rigging Sight-Cast Leaders"*).

2. "Chumming With Light Spin Or Plug Tackle"

Once you've located a school of dolphin by trolling, light spinning tackle and small chunks of bait can be substituted. This method gives the angler a chance to use light spin and conserves the use of expensive ballyhoo on school fish. It's best to have chunks of ballyhoo and the tackle standing by before the school is found.

Save your worn trolling baits or old bait for chumming. Take the ballyhoo and cut cross-sections 1 inch wide. Each ballyhoo makes five baits. Use the head and tail for chum.

Eight- to 15-pound-test spin tackle works well. A 4-foot leader of 50-pound test and a #3704 Mustad 5/0 hook will allow you to lift school-sized dolphin into the boat without breaking the line (See: *"Appendix D-1"*).

It's usually best to drift while fishing a school. Always keep one dolphin in the water to hold the interest of the school. Once a school of dolphin is located one dolphin must remain hooked on the trolling tackle while the trolling lines are cleared.

Another fish should be hooked on the light spin and several chunks of chum dispersed before boating the dolphin on the trolling rod. Rotate boating the dolphin in the order hooked on the light tackle. Freshly-hooked dolphin also regurgitate minnows to help you chum.

36. Catching school dolphin on light spin tackle.

3. "Tailing Dolphin"

The term "tailing" came from Miami, where sailfish swimming down sea and into the current on a north wind expose half of their tails as they glide down the swells. Many species of gamefish will tail, swimming down sea using the upper cyclonic energy of the waves to assist them as they swim into the current.

Tailing can occur when the wind is blowing into the current regardless of the direction of the current or wind. These fish are not aggressive feeders and will glide right past trolled baits without giving the bait a second look.

Using the sight-cast and flying fish reflex techniques with dead ballyhoo or flying fish on a spinner will attract strikes from most tailing dolphin. Live bait is not necessary. Generally, when dolphin will begin to follow baits on a north wind but not strike, casting directly to the fish will excite them into feeding (See: *"Sight-Casting to Dolphin"* Chapter XIII-1).

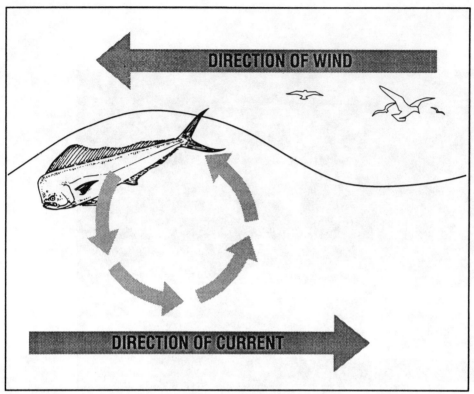

37. Dolphin tailing, when the wind opposes the current

4. "Using the Deep-Troll (Downrigger) to Catch Dolphin"

Dolphin generally feed on the surface and respond to surface baits. But, there are certain weather, wind and current conditions which all but eliminate surface feeding. Under these conditions, dolphin are reluctant feeders and you will only catch two or three fish from any one school. But, using the deep-troll will save you from getting skunked when dolphin stop surface feeding.

Conditions which reduce dolphin feeding activity include:

•*Northerly winds*
Winds north of 90° East cool surface temperatures and break up weedlines abruptly, stopping dolphin surface-feeding.

•*Upwelling currents*
Upwelling currents can be caused by several factors: movements of the

Special Fishing Techniques

Gulf Stream, unusual currents and El Nino. Upwelling also cools surface temperatures, abruptly stopping surface feeding.

• *Upper-level, non-tropical low pressure systems*
These weather systems are characterized by high-level, gray skies that reduce light and create upwelling currents, slowing dolphin surface feeding. However, tropical low pressure systems can bring a bonanza of dolphin activity.

The deep-troll (downrigger) can be used in any of the above conditions to take a bait down to where the dolphin are in the water column. Size the baits properly to attract dolphin strikes, then run the line down to a depth of 30 to 60 feet.

Dolphin hooked on deep troll will bring other dolphin to the surface baits where additional hook-ups can occur. Place the deep-troll bait at a distance where the release on hook-up will bring fish near the top lines (See: *"Dolphin on the deep-troll"* Appendix G-3).

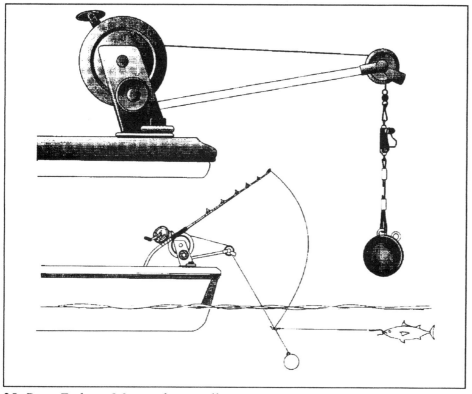

38. Penn Fathom-Master deep-troll.

5. "Fishing in Sargassum Seaweed"

Fishing in or around sargassum seaweed can be very easy when the wind and current have lined up the sargassum in a nice, straight weedline or pushed the seaweed into giant patches, leaving the angler lots of clean water around the seaweed to troll in. This, however, is not always the case. Sometimes the seaweed can be scattered, tangling trolled baits. I have developed several techniques to make trolling in and around seaweed easy and productive.

Trolling rigged baits (ballyhoo, flying fish, mullet, etc.) works well when large dolphin are concentrated. Artificials have an advantage on lines loaded with small school dolphin, enabling the angler to size up lures to catch the larger dolphin.

Trolling in scattered grass presents a whole new problem: How do you keep grass off the baits long enough to catch fish?

Weedless artificial lures

Certain artificial lures resist catching grass and others simply can't be used in grass. Our "Sea Boots" Kona lure was designed to troll at high speed and not catch grass. Mold Craft Soft Heads, R&S TAE and Talisman lures are other examples of lures that resist catching grass (See: *"Weedless Lures"* Appendix C-3).

Hook size and lure design must match to prevent fouling with sargassum. The hook should be smaller than the lure-head's largest diameter and be covered by the skirts. In the case of the Kona lure, the small diameter of the head allows water pressure to dislodge the grass and the skirts protect the hook.

Weedless rigged baits

Both single- and double-hooked ballyhoo pin-rigs can be modified to troll in scattered grass conditions without catching grass. This technique is so simple it took me over 20 years to develop it! Take a single-hook ballyhoo trolling rig and turn the pin around 180°. Place the pin through the head of the ballyhoo and put the single, #3407 ring-eye hook into the bait (the same as a double-hook pin rig). Slant the pin slightly backward and wrap the ballyhoo's bill with copper wire so that no snags are created where the leader meets the bill (See: *"Appendix B-3"*).

There is one down-side to the single-hook weedless rig – you will not be able to hook a billfish on it. Billfish don't tear baits, they crush and swallow them whole. The weedless bait will just pull right out of their mouths. **Suggestion**: Keep a double-hook rig with the last hook exposed handy to hook a billfish should one appear.

39. Sargassum seaweed.

Chapter XIV

Hooking, Fighting, Leadering and Gaffing Dolphin

1. "Hooking and Fighting Dolphin"

A dropback is necessary when trying to hook sailfish but not with dolphin. Given the aggressive nature of dolphin, most of the time they will hook themselves on a trolling bait. Dropping back to dolphin usually results in the fish eating two of your trolled baits.

Dolphin that are reluctant to eat, but follow the bait, can be teased by raising and lowering the rod, giving the bait more action. When the fish moves in for the kill, just drop the rod tip to allow 2 or 3 feet of slack for the hook-up without free spooling the reel.

Set the hook with a tight line by pumping up on the rod, lifting firmly and smoothly, approximately 8 to 10 inches, keeping the rod at a 45° angle, and repeating three or four times. No hay-bailers or bass-snatchers, please. Maintaining the proper rod angle during the hook-up is accomplished by winding quickly if necessary, not by lifting the rod to a higher angle in an attempt to take up slack. Never lift the rod higher than the 45° angle and never point the rod at the fish. If the line isn't tight, wind quickly until tight then set the hook.

Hooking dolphin when sight-casting or using chunks on school fish is quite different from trolling. The angler must take charge of getting the line tight during the hook-up without the forward motion of the boat. Dolphin bite down hard on their prey before swallowing them, so long dropbacks can decrease the number of hook-ups rather than increase them. During long dropbacks the dolphin becomes aware of the hook and drops the bait.

Dolphin: The Perfect Gamefish

I have found that the greatest percentage of hook-ups occur when the hook is set as soon as the dolphin eats the bait. The angler must watch the dolphin eat the bait or feel the movement of the line to know when to set the hook. First wind out the slack until the line comes tight then, with the rod at a 45° angle, set the hook using three to four 10-inch pumps.

Hooked dolphin will make a fast surface run and then begin jumping, it's important to keep the line tight and the rod loaded at the 45° angle. The line can be kept tight by winding. DO NOT pull back on the rod to tighten the line.

After a series of jumps and runs, big dolphin will cruise near the surface. They tend to pull at angles to the resistance of the line using their wide heads and the drag of the water against you. The angler can respond by pulling left with the rod as the fish goes to the right, the pull right as the fish swims left. This keeps the dolphin from just coasting.

Big dolphin often sound at the boat, staying 20 or 30 feet below the surface. These fish will slowly spiral, using their wide heads to create drag against the angler's pull. This requires little energy burn on the part of the fish but the angler begins to fight himself and the pressure of the water.

This spiral must be broken so the fish will have to burn energy. The angler can break the spiral by using a short pump-and-wind technique. Lift the fish's head 6 inches and wind down quickly and carefully so you don't lose the line gained. This is when the angler's skills are paramount. Get into a smooth rhythm, lifting and winding in a manner that no line is lost to the fish and the dolphin is forced upward. Once the dolphin realizes it is no longer in control, it will bolt for the surface and jump. Keep the pressure on with normal pump-and-wind techniques and the dolphin will be yours.

2. "Wind-On Leaders"

Aboard our charter boats, *"Sea Boots 43"* and *"Sea Boots 34"*, we use two monofilament sizes for leaders. Most of the summer we use 80-pound mono, but when the dolphin get picky or the tuna show up we use 50- or 60-pound mono leaders. You will definitely get more strikes on the smaller leaders (50- to 60-pound) but the 80-pound leaders are more chafe-resistant and offer better durability if you hook-up with a big dolphin or other big gamefish such as tuna, sailfish, white or blue marlin. Fluorocarbon leaders are expensive, but offer more strikes and greater durability.

Trying to control larger gamefish on light leaders at the boat demanded we change our techniques from traditional leaders to wind-ons, which we have now been using for many years. The wind-on leader consists of double-line tied with a Bimini twist, with the leader tied directly to the double-line using an Albright knot. The snap swivel is tied in the leader 6 to 8 feet above the bait. This allows the angler to wind both the double-line and the wind-on part of the leader onto the reel up to the snap swivel (See: *"Appendices A-1 & 2"*).

The wind-on leader allows the angler to control the fish right to the point where the mate can gaff or tag the fish without pulling on the leader. The distance between the snap swivel and the bait can be adjusted to fit any size boat. Wind-on leaders prevent broken lines when fish suddenly bolt and minimize dangers of mates being dragged overboard and possibly drowned while trying to leader the fish.

3. "Leadering and Gaffing Dolphin"

Even if you are using a wind-on leader it is important to handle the leader correctly during the gaffing process. Dolphin jump when threatened so the mate must control the leader as the fish nears the boat, holding the leader low to the water until the fish can be reached with the gaff. This keeps the fish calm and in the water for the gaff shot.

During gaffing, reach over the top and beyond the dolphin, aiming approximately 10 inches behind the head and pull with the gaff hook pointed down. The captain should keep the vessel moving forward slowly during the gaffing process. After placing the gaff, keep the fish out of the water and bring the dolphin into the boat. Assign one angler to sit on the cooler or fish box lid to prevent the dolphin from kicking off the lid and jumping overboard. Tend the rod and reel until the leader is detached or the hook is removed from the fish.

I recommend two gaff sizes: One, a 2-inch hook on a 4-foot, solid fiberglass rod blank makes a light-weight gaff that can be maneuvered easily in the water when gaffing large-school to medium-size dolphin. Second, a 4- or 6-inch hook on a 7- to 8-foot wood or aluminum pole for gaffing dolphin weighing more than 20 pounds (See: "Gaffs" Appendix H-2).

40. Mate keeps the leader low to prevent the dolphin from jumping.

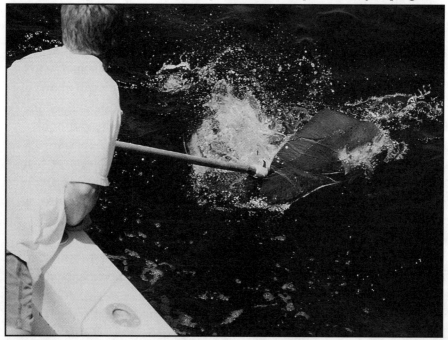

41. Mate reaches over and pulls back on the gaff.

Chapter XV
Fly Fishing for Dolphin

1. "Dolphin On The Fly"

Dolphin are the perfect gamefish on any tackle: Spectacular jumpers, lighting-fast runs and plenty of down-and-dirty. Fighting dolphin on fly tackle is just a blast, they tend to jump more and really wear themselves out fighting the fly line. The long rod and heavy water-drag on the fly line combine to wear out the fish quickly.

To be productive, the flyfishing technique must match the dolphin's feeding patterns. I recommend two techniques for catching dolphin on the fly; For dolphin feeding on flying fish in open blue water, *"Trolling and Teasing"* works best. For dolphin schooling around boards or weedlines I recommend the *"Dead-Boat Casting"* technique.

2. "Trolling and Teasing"

The most common method for raising big game such as billfish to the fly is trolling with hookless teasers, baits or lures until the fish rise into the baits. This method is not accepted by many flats guides but, in the open expanses of the ocean, it can be one of the angler's only options for finding fish. To be legal by International Game Fish Association standards, the fly must be cast and the fish hooked while the boat is out of gear.

Once dolphin are sighted in the trolling pattern, they are teased into position by winding a hookless teaser bait/lure into range of the fly. The boat is pulled out of gear and the angler presents the fly using a snap cast. The angler must be ready to deliver the fly to the dolphin trailing the teaser (See: *"Teasing"* Appendix F-2).

Before the dolphin is raised on the teaser, the angler strips off enough fly line to position the fly just in front of the teasers. Then the fly line is stripped back into the boat allowing fly line to lie naturally on the deck. Some anglers prefer to strip the fly line into a basket. This will insure that, during the snap cast, the fly end of the line will come off the top of the line coil to preventing tangling.

To execute the snap cast, leave 1½ rod-lengths of fly line outside the tip. Standing in the stern corner of the boat, hold the fly lightly between the thumb and index finger. Snap the fly rod back, preventing the fly line from moving with the index finger of the rod hand. The thumb and index finger hold the fly firmly until the fast-moving line snatches the fly from your fingers. As the rod loads, the forward cast is made. With a little practice, this method can deliver the fly to the fish in a matter of seconds. If the desired distance is not obtained, lift the fly and cast again. Double hauling can increase distance and accuracy if needed.

The fly is presented slightly in front of and to the near side of the striking gamefish. The angler points the rod at the fly, stripping the fly using short, 6-inch strips. When the dolphin strikes and tension is felt on the line, pull down on the fly line with the left hand and up on the rod with the right hand to set the hook. Take care to get the line back on the reel without tangling objects in the boat.

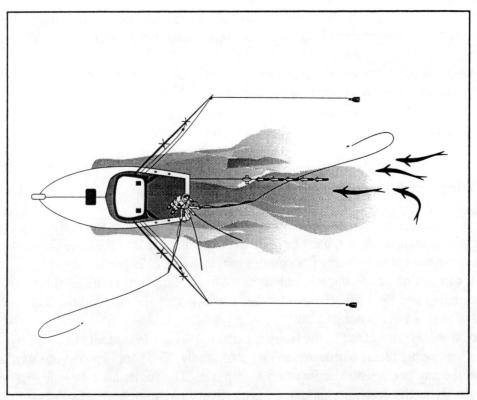

42. Using the "snap cast" to present the fly to dolphin after teasing.

3. "Dead-Boat Casting"

The dead-boat method is an option for fly casting to dolphin around floating objects. The boat should be positioned slightly up-wind at a 90-degree angle to the direction of the wind. In this position, the angler doesn't have to drive the fly line into the wind on either the back cast or the forecast and the fly line will drift away from the angler during the cast. The angler can cast from either the cockpit or the bow but should carefully select his location, avoiding objects that would foul the fly line.

Keep a spinning rod with hookless plug or bait standing by to cast and tease dolphin away from the weeds into the range of the fly if necessary (See: *"Appendix F"*). For dolphin that don't want to eat the fly, the mate can cast the teaser out and retrieve it at a fast rate of speed to excite the fish

The mate lays the fly out in the path of the teaser, allowing it to settle as the teaser is retrieved. When the dolphin, hot on the trail of the teaser, approaches the fly, the mate quickly pulls the teaser out of the water with a long stroke and the angler strips the fly right in the dolphin's face (See: *"Appendix F"*).

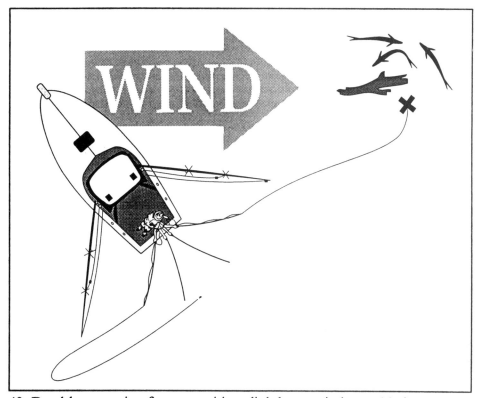

43. Dead-boat casting from a position slightly up-wind, at a 90-degree angle to the wind

4. "Teasing Dolphin with a Kite"

A fishing kite can be used for teasing gamefish prior to presenting the fly. The neat thing about teasing dolphin with a live bait from a kite is that, after the fish is excited, the live bait can be lifted up out of the water and the fly presented. If the dolphin loses interest, drop the bait back down in the water and tease the fish again (See: *"Kites"* Appendix F).

5. "Fly Tackle and Rigging"

For small dolphin (schoolies) a seven- to eight-weight fly rod and reel will offer a lot of fun. I recommend the eight-weight-forward, floating fly line with 4 feet of 30-pound monofilament line for the butt section. The class tippet can be 4- to 12-pound test with a 10-inch, 30-pound test monofilament shock tippet to protect against chafing at the fly.

For medium-size dolphin, 10 to 25 pounds, I recommend a nine- to 10-weight fly rod and reel. Use a weight-forward, floating 10-weight fly line with a 4- foot butt section of 50-pound monofilament line. The line-class tippet should be 8- to 16-pound test with 10 inches of 50-pound shock tippet for chafing protection at the fly (See: *Appendix F*).

For large dolphin, 25 to 40 pounds, I recommend an 8- to 9-foot, 12-weight, Penn or G-Loomis rod and a 12-weight fly reel with a large disc-drag system such as Penn or Islander with 250 yards or more of 30-pound-test backing. Anti-reverse or direct drive is a matter of personal preference. The fly line should be a weight-forward-floating 12-weight with a 4-foot butt section of 80-pound test mono-filament. The line-class tippet can range from 12- to 20-pound. A 10-inch shock tippet of 80-pound test monofilament must be used to prevent chafing (See: *"Fly lines and leaders"* Appendix F).

Small epoxy minnow flies with 2/0 hooks are durable and work well for small dolphin. Most popper flies or tarpon flies with 2/0 to 4/0 hooks work well for medium, size dolphin. For big dolphin I recommend Captain Lenny Moffo's blue and white Big Boy fly with two 4/0 hooks.

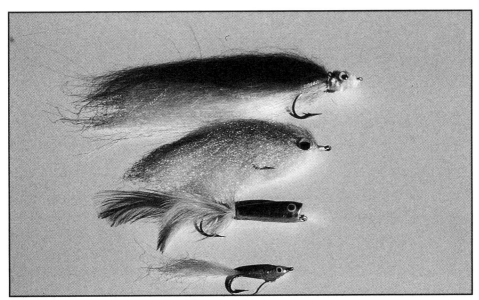

44. Selection of flies for catching dolphin.

DOLPHIN FISHING ETIQUETTE

There are times when several boats can work together on schools of dolphin and times when other boats should stand clear. It is *"not"* okay to troll past a boat drift-fishing a school of dolphin. Here's what happens: By trolling past, you draw the school to the movement of your boat and away from the drifting boat. You hook several dolphin, pull the fish into the boat and the entire school swims away and is lost.

If you are invited over, pull up and drift with the other boat. The school will stay with both boats and everybody can catch fish. Quite often the action created by two boats drift-fishing dolphin will drawn more dolphin from surrounding waters than one would.

Running from boat to boat hoping to share their school is not acceptable sportsmanship either. There are times when dolphin are around floating objects in great numbers and it's okay to join the action, but if there are only a few fish, stand clear.

Chasing dolphin under birds also has some rules of fair play: Don't try to race other boats to birds. Boats closest to the birds should have the first pass. If the dolphin are coming through under birds there will be other schools, you don't have to fight over one.

When joining other boats on a weedline don't run up in front of another boat. Its more polite to fish the weedline in the other direction or fish along side boats already working the line.

APPENDICES

****
SUMMARY
****

Fishing is a practice, not a science. Applying the information in this book will get easier as the angler gains experience. Since multiple factors such as wind speed, wind direction, tide, moon phase and season often come into play, the angler must weigh the importance of each factor and predict the outcome. A plan of action may change as conditions change during the fishing day. The following tips summarize some of the major points in this book.

POMPANO VS COMMON DOLPHIN

•A dolphin can be identified by size of the widest point of its body. In common dolphin the widest point is the head, while the pompano is widest at the middle of the body.

•Pompano dolphin are more oceanic than common dolphin and rarely grow to more than 8 pounds.

•Pompano dolphin are found only where surface temperatures reach above 75.2° Fahrenheit.

•Common dolphin do not occur in waters with surface temperatures below 69.8° Fahrenheit.

WINDS, TIDES AND CURRENTS

• Factors that bring aggressive dolphin feeding include wind in the southeasterly quadrant, favorable moon phase and strong flow of the Gulf Stream.

•Factors that cause passive dolphin feeding include northerly winds, bright nights and slow Gulf Stream current.

Dolphin: The Perfect Gamefish

• Dolphin feed aggressively on the bright nights of the full moon, but daytime feeding will be passive.

• The most aggressive daytime bite will come on building tides preceding the bright nights of the full moon and several days preceding the new moon.

• Weedlines and rips usually form in the Florida Keys coastal area on outgoing tides with winds in the southeasterly quadrant.

• Incoming tides in the coastal area usually scatter weedlines and rips.

• Winds in the northerly quadrant scatter and disperse weedlines and rips.

• The major offshore feeding period for dolphin is from 11:00 a.m. to 2:00 p.m.

• Daytime minor feeding periods occur from 4:00 p.m. to 6:00 p.m. around the time of the full moon.

• On coastal tidal rips that occur inside of 400 feet of water, major dolphin feeding periods can occur from daylight to 11:00 a.m. particularly on a falling tide.

• Schools of migrating dolphin tend to continue moving in the direction of the migration.

• Spring migrations of dolphin move in a northerly direction while fall migrations move in a southerly direction.

FISHING TIPS

• Small baits and lures catch both large and small dolphin. Use larger baits and lures to target only larger fish.

• To keep a school near the boat, hold the most recently hooked dolphin in the water until another fish is hooked.

RIGGING FOR DOLPHIN

A. Setting up the wind-on leader

1. Double-line, leader and knots

The double-line is formed by doubling the main line and tying a Bimini twist knot. A spider-hitch knot can also be used but offers only 80 percent of the breaking strength of the line. The Bimini breaks at more than 100 percent line strength. The double line should be 1 foot long for every 10 pounds of line test. For example: 30-pound-test line should have a 3-foot double line. The double line acts as a shock absorber, preventing line failure from sudden stress.

A Sharpe's/Albright knot is used to tie a 15-foot monofilament leader into the double-line. Refer to IGFA standard leader lengths for different sizes of tackle. A Coastal lock swivel for trolling baits or lures can be tied to the terminal end of the leader, or use a live-bait hook for sight-casting to dolphin.

2. Trolling leader for baits or lures

The wind-on leader for trolling is essentially the same as the wind-on leader for sight-casting except for the terminal end. In the case of the trolling leader a Coastal lock swivel is added at the end of the leader and 6 to 8 feet additional leader is used for trolling baits and lures.

A surgeon's knot is used to form an eye to attach to the Coastal lock swivel. I recommend the surgeon's knot over the much neater looking uni-knot. The uni-knot, developed by Vic Dunaway to connect fishing lines or snell a hook – not to form a loop – will sometimes fail even when tied correctly. A 6- to 8-foot leader with rigged ballyhoo or lure can be changed quickly by just un-snapping the Coastal lock and snapping on a new bait or lure.

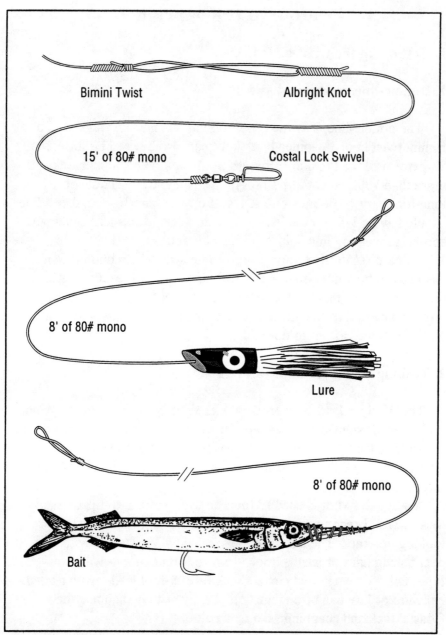

Bimini Twist

Albright Knot

15' of 80# mono

Costal Lock Swivel

8' of 80# mono

Lure

8' of 80# mono

Bait

45. The wind-on leader and trolling leaders for baits or lures

3. Spin or plug, sight-casting leaders

On the sight-casting leader, the hook is attached directly at the terminal end of the leader. There is no swivel. This allows the angler to wind up and fire the bait out when dolphin are sighted without worrying about the swivel. When sight-casting to dolphin I prefer a 8/0 ring-eye #3704 Mustad hook sharpened with a file. The hook is passed through the top of the ballyhoo's head and the shank of the hook secured to the ballyhoo's bill with soft, copper wrapping wire. For flying fish or live baits the hook can be passed through the head.

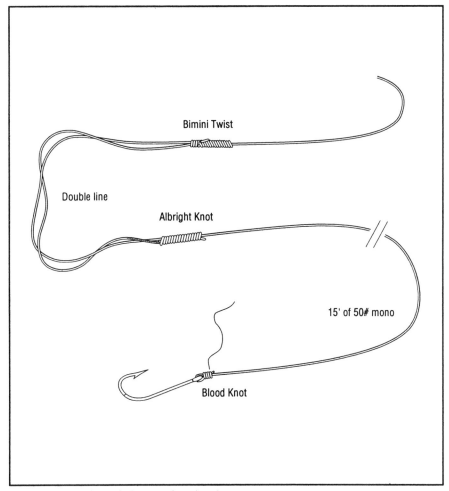

46. Spin or plug sight-casting leaders.

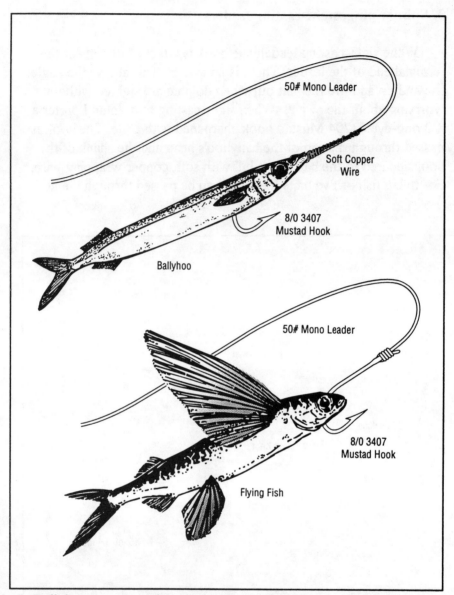

47. Ballyhoo are secured to the hook with soft copper wire while live baits or flying fish are simply hooked thru the head.

4. Standby big-game tackle

While you are dolphin fishing, other exciting sportfishing opportunities can present themselves. For example, you may be enjoying some light-tackle fishing with a school of dolphin around the boat when suddenly a big marlin or mako shark joins in. Now is not the time to try and get ready, the tackle should be ready and waiting. I recommend having a Penn 50W or 80W standing by, rigged with a wind-on leader and a #3277, 11/0 stainless-steel marlin hook. A live school dolphin can be used to bait the feeding marlin or shark. Being ready is the key to success.

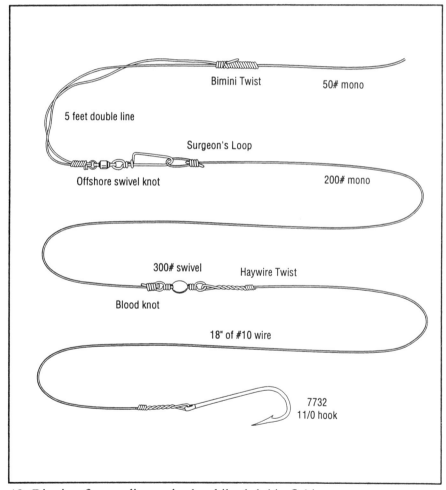

48. Rigging for marlin or shark while dolphin fishing

B. "Rigging Trolling Baits"

1. Single-hook baits

Single-hook baits are used for dolphin, tuna and billfish. When rigged with care, they troll naturally through the water, swimming upright like a live fish. The single-hook ballyhoo can be rigged with wire, cable or monofilament leader. I recommend rigging surface lines with mono leaders. Even though you will occasionally lose a nice wahoo or other toothy fish the mono will consistently draw more strikes. The deep-troll will draw most of the wahoo and kingfish strikes. Here I recommend the double-hook bait. To rig the single-hook ballyhoo, first make the leader and pin-rig with soft copper wire. *(Illustration B-1.)*

49. The ballyhoo monofilament single-hook trolling rig.

To make the bait, first measure the pin and hook position. Using the point of the hook make a small puncture in the stomach where the hook should exit.

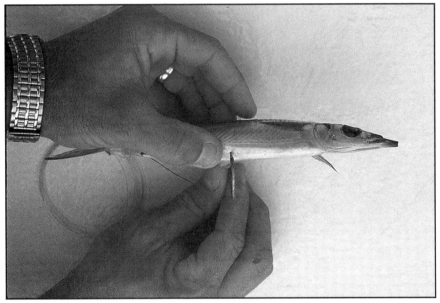

50. Measuring and marking the position of the hook.

Then pass the 8/0, #3407 ring-eye hook through the gill of the bally-hoo into the stomach cavity and out through the stomach at the puncture.

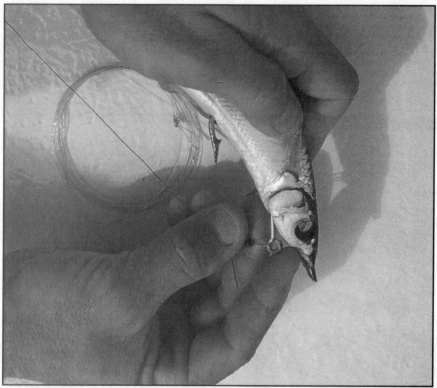

51. Bring the hook out the marked spot.

After the hook is placed, push the pin up through the head as shown and secure the pin and leader with copper wrapping wire.

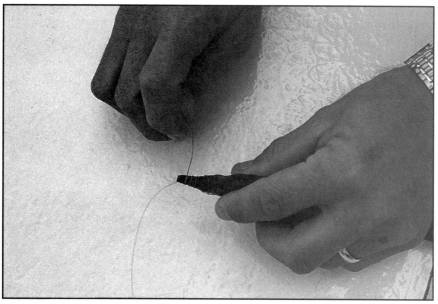

52. Securing the pin and bill with copper wrapping wire.

Dolphin: **The Perfect Gamefish**

All trolling baits must pull by the pin or they will spin. An improperly-placed hook is one thing that will make a bait spin. Solution: Make a small relief cut next to the hook.

53. Relief cut at the hook – a solution to a spinning bait.

An off-center pin in the fish head or a leader secured off center will also make a bait spin. Adjust pin and leader and test. Test all rigged baits by trolling them close to the boat to insure they don't spin before setting the trolling pattern.

2. Double-Hook Baits

Double-hook baits resist most cut-offs by wahoo and kings and work well on the deep-troll where most wahoo strikes occur. They are also weedless by the nature of the rig and work well in heavy scattered grass. (For surface trolling for dolphin in heavy scattered grass, I recommend the single-hook weedless ballyhoo discussed under weedless baits.) Double-hook baits fished on the deep-troll set at 50 feet below the surface will produce most of the strikes on a northerly wind and in upwelling conditions.

To make the double-hook rig, the pin is pushed up through the ballyhoo's head and secured.

54. Securing the pin in the double-hook ballyhoo rig.

The first hook is measured and pushed into the stomach from the outside. The second hook is allowed to hang free.

55. Placing the first hook into the bait.

3. Weedless baits

Trolling around neatly-formed patches of sargassum is no problem, but when wind and tide scatter the grass over large areas, weedless baits are a must. The single-hook weedless ballyhoo rig is the best surface bait to use in heavy scattered weeds. The single-hook weed-less ballyhoo is made exactly like the double-hook rig, using only one 8/0, #3407 ring-eye hook. Secure the leader and pin into the ballyhoo, then measure and place the single hook into the stomach from the outside. Use the relief cut if necessary.

56. Single-hook ballyhoo weedless bait.

This dolphin bait is excellent used in scattered grass conditions. However, it will not hook a hungry billfish. A dolphin breaks the bait on strike, exposing the hook. Billfish do not break the bait so the hook stays in the bait and can't hook the billfish.

With this in mind, I recommend trolling three single-hook, weedless ballyhoo and one double-hook ballyhoo on the flat line. The double-hook ballyhoo bait is weedless and will hook billfish because the second hook is exposed.

C. "Rigging Trolling Lures"

1. Single-hook lures

Most lures are rigged with single hooks. The hook is placed at the back of the lure for the best hook-ups. A ¼-ounce sliding sinker can be used to move the hook back in the lure if necessary. Slide the sinker on the leader between the hook and the lure adjust hook and crimp or mash the sinker to maintain hook position in the lure.

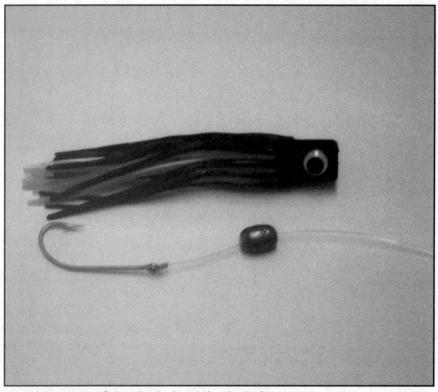

57. Placement of the single-hook in the bait.

118

To determine the proper hook-size for a lure, compare the hook to the diameter of the lure's head. The distance across the hook from tip to shank should roughly equal the diameter of the lure head.

58. Selecting the proper size hook for the lure.

2. Double-Hook Lures

I recommend double-hooks for larger lures like the Sea Boots Kona lure to protect against cut-offs in case a wahoo strikes. A pair of ring-eye, #3407 Mustad hooks are joined by bending the eye of the trailing hook open and linking the two facing in opposite directions.

This lure and double-hook set-up works well in heavy grass and will catch a variety of gamefish including those with teeth.

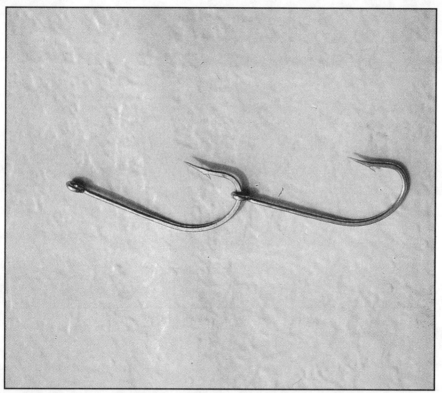

59. Bending two hooks together to make double hooks.

3. Weedless Lures

The shape and diameter of the lure-head, plus proper rigging and hook selection determine how well the lure will perform under heavy grass conditions. Lures that I use to avoid the most grass include the Mold Craft Little Hooker ll00P, Standard Hooker 4450H, Senior Hooker 3450H, the Talisman Little Smoker and the Kona by Sea Boots Outfitters. The Sea Boots Kona is the best weedless lure I have seen and will attract larger dolphin, wahoo and billfish. The dolphin's keen sense of prey size must always be considered when selecting lures.

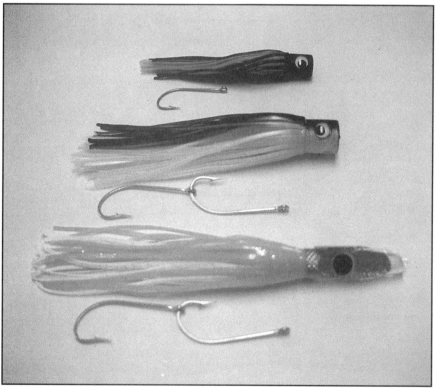

60. Lures to avoid grass and catch dolphin

D. "Rigging Light Tackle"

1. Chumming school dolphin

School dolphin are fun to catch on light spin or plug tackle. The leader begins with a 60-pound barrel swivel tied directly to the main line, followed by a 4-foot, 50-pound-test monofilament leader tied to a 5/0, #3407 Mustad hook. The 4-foot leader allows the angler to lift dolphin into the boat without breaking the line.

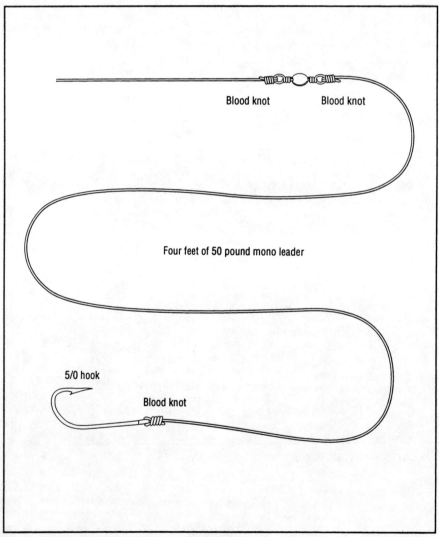

Blood knot   Blood knot

Four feet of 50 pound mono leader

5/0 hook

Blood knot

61. A leader for chumming school dolphin.

I recommend using the Sharpe's Blood Knot – a knot taught to me by my father in 1950 – at the swivel and hook. With a 76-year proven history in my family I don't experiment with other knots.

The Sharpe's Blood Knot is very similar to the clinch knot. Pass the line through the eye of the hook and pass the tag end over the main line, forming an eye. With the thumb and index finger of the left hand, freeze the eye in the line in a horizontal position.

Using the right hand, wrap the tag end of the line around the main line six times, do not let the eye move. Pass the tag end of the line from below up through the frozen eye and pull the knot down tight. If the eye moves or slips out of your fingers start all over.

To tie an Improved Sharpe's Blood Knot, after passing the tag end through the frozen eye, the tag end can be passed through the larger loop before pulling the knot tight similar to the Improved Clinch Knot. This does not improve the strength of the knot but makes tightening the knot easier in some applications, such as tying line to the spool of a reel. The knot can be tied above the spool, tightened then slid down onto the spool.

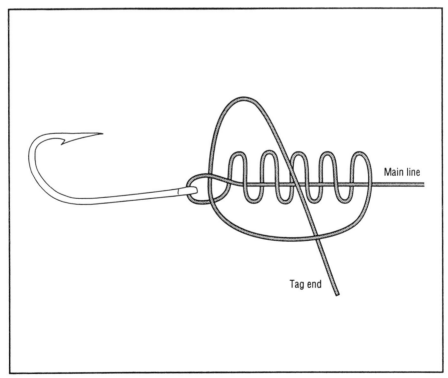

Main line

Tag end

62. Sharpe's Blood Knot

Don't pass the tag end through from the top rather than the bottom of the frozen eye. It changes the lay of the line resulting in a knot that tests well under steady pressure but will pull out under sudden stress. A small curly-cue in the broken end of the line after sudden line-failure indicates a pulled knot. If the knot strength equals the line test, line breaks will occur in mid-line, leaving the knot on the hook, swivel etc. There will be no curly-cue at the terminal end of the line.

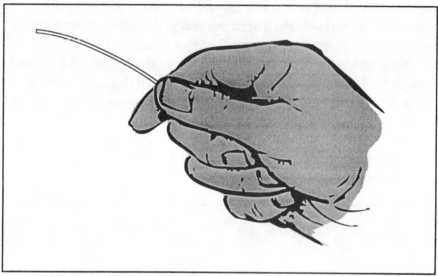

63. Line Failure

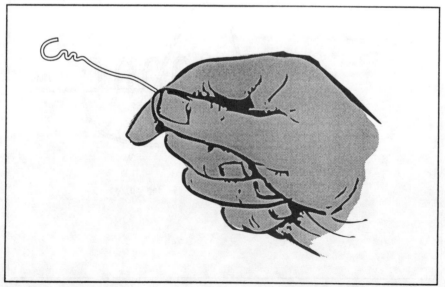

64. Knot Failure

2. Casting Jigs/Plugs with Plug or Spin Tackle.

Use caution when casting jigs or plugs around dolphin. Dolphin are great jumpers and will throw artificials. The bent rod propels the artificial back into the boat with enough force to drive the hook into you. I recommend using the 5/0 hook and small piece of bait – it's less dangerous. If you just enjoy casting to fish, try using a epoxy-head fly or tarpon fly on spin tackle. With less weight there is less recoil when the hook is thrown.

For casters using plug tackle, I recommend the Bagley Finger Mullet, MirrOlure 51M sinker or a 7M 24 floater plug – but make some alterations before fishing. Remove the front and middle treble hooks from the plug completely. Then remove and replace the rear treble with a 1/0 or 2/0, #9174 live-bait hook using a Rosco, Size One split ring to attach the hook to the eye in the rear of the plug. The plug will work just as well and it reduces the possibility of painful injury when the plug returns into the boat during the un-hooking process.

I highly recommend using the un-hooker shown in *Appendix H* on all dolphin.

65. Plug with treble hooks removed.

Dolphin: The Perfect Gamefish

Refer to *Appendix A-3* for rigging leaders for 15 to 20 pound test spin or plug gear. When using lighter tackle the angler must consider hook size and leader size. While 8/0 hooks are appropriate for 20-pound tackle, this size hook is impossible to set with 6- to 12-pound tackle. Instead, a 1/0 to 4//0 hook is more appropriate for 6- to 12-pound tackle. The angler should also refer to the IGFA World Record Game Fishes book for legal double-line and leader requirements for world records.

E. "Rigging Teasers for Trolling with Baits or Lures"

Teasers are very important when trolling for dolphin. One of my favorites is the squid teaser with a bird. A small Mold Craft bird followed by five or six, 6-inch squid are arranged 1 foot apart on a 10-foot section of 150-pound monofilament. Mix up the colors for contrast. The teaser is towed 30-feet astern on a heavy line and must be pulled out of the water quickly after the hook-up. It is important to arrange baits around the teaser so that fish drawn to the teaser can find the baits easily.

66. Bird/squid teaser.

F. "Fly Fishing for Dolphin"

1. Rigging fly tackle

a. **Fly line:** I recommend weight-forward, floating or intermediate fly line like the Cortland Big Game taper 444sl. The short front taper, only 24 feet, helps to turn over large salt water flies and pulls running line through for longer casts. The floating line floats high in the water for easy pick up, but on very calm days the intermediate fly line is slightly more dense and settles just below the surface and doesn't make a wake when stripping. These salt water lines are tough, with a durable coating to resist chaffing, and cast easily. Most offshore fly fisherman cut 15 to 20 feet off the back of the fly line to increase the amount of backing on the reel.

b. **Fly leader, butt section, line class tippet and shock leader:** The butt section is generally four feet in length and is tied to the fly line using a nail knot. At the other end of the butt section a loop is formed with a surgeon's loop. The line-class tippet must be more than 15 inches in length, a Bimini twist knot is tied at each end of the tippet. The butt section is looped to one end of a Bimini twist built into the tippet. At the other end of the tippet the shock tippet is tied into the Bimini twist with an Albright/Sharpe Knot. The fly is then tied to the shock tippet with a Sharpe's Blood Knot or Homer Rhode Loop Knot. Some anglers prefer the Uni-knot which allows the fly and hook to swing freely on the loop that's formed.

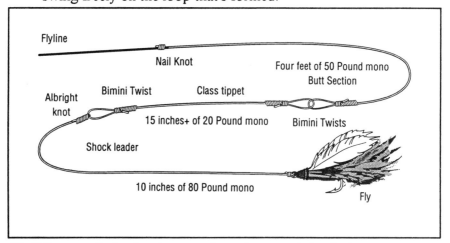

67. Saltwater fly leader: butt section, tippet and shock tippet.

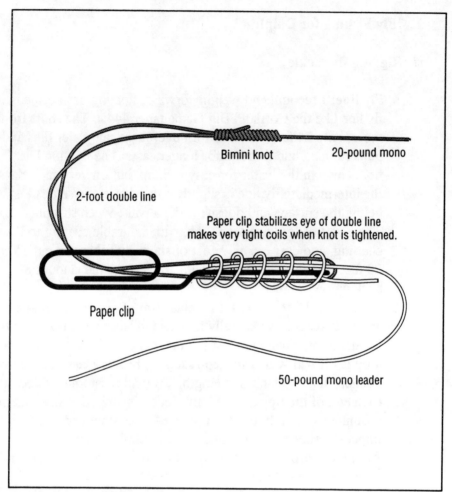

Bimini knot 20-pound mono

2-foot double line

Paper clip stabilizes eye of double line
makes very tight coils when knot is tightened.

Paper clip

50-pound mono leader

68. Sharpe's Albright Knot

2. Troll/Tease fly casting

The Cortland Big Game Taper salt water fly line pays off here.
The short front taper will turn over the fly line and larger flies while
pulling off running line with a tight loop when using the snap cast for
quick delivery from the cockpit to the gamefish. Remember the boat is
at trolling speed when the fish is teased into the baits – then the boat is
pulled out of gear for the presentation of the fly. The forward momen-
tum of the boat helps the angler by pulling off running line and give
the fly added action on the strip. (Refer to *Appendix F-4* for more
information on rigging fly-fishing teasers for Troll/Teasing dolphin.)

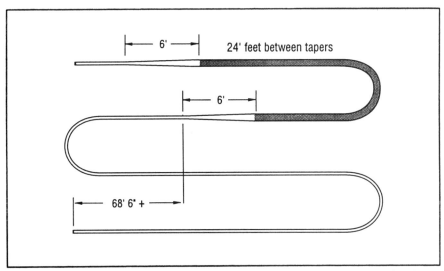

6'

24' feet between tapers

6'

68' 6" +

69. Cortland 444sl Big Game taper (Floating or Intermediate) fly line has a short front taper to turn over large flies. The 24-foot body pulls running line through for longer casts.

3. Dead-boat fly casting

After the boat is located in the proper position in relation to the flotsam or jetsam, 12- to 20-pound-test spin or plug tackle can be used to tease and attract dolphin into position for fly casting. This is done by casting a hookless plug near the fish and retrieving it to the boat. The gamefish will follow the teaser to the boat and the fly fisherman presents the fly when the gamefish is within casting distance. There is little chance of tangling with the spin or plug-cast teaser because there is no hook. I recommend using the MirrOlure 51M 24 Sinker or the Bagley Finger Mullet because the line is attached to the nose of the plug rather than the top of the head. This will tend to jump over the fly line and not tangle.

4. Rigging teasers for fly fishing

Teasers are used to attract gamefish within range of the fly caster. This can be accomplished by several methods: Trolling-and-teasing, casting with hookless artificials with spin or plug tackle from a drifting boat or teasing with a live or dead bait suspended from a kite.

a. Rigging teasers for trolling and snap fly casting: Artificials or live or dead bait can be used for teasing while trolling. I prefer using artificials. The artificial teaser consists of five 6-inch Mold Craft squid spaced 18 inches apart with a Mold Craft Little Bird heading up the parade. Five Mold Craft Little Hookers 1100 P with Little Bird also make a good teaser. The MoldCraft Medium Hooker 4450 H with the Standard Bird works well for larger dolphin.

Rig the Squid or Hookers and bird on a 15-foot length of 50-pound monofilament line with a 150-pound barrel swivel. Eighth-inch braided nylon rope makes a good main line to the boat. Quarter-ounce lead sinkers can be mashed onto the mono behind each squid/hooker/bird to hold them in place. (See: Appendix E *Bird/Squid teaser*.)

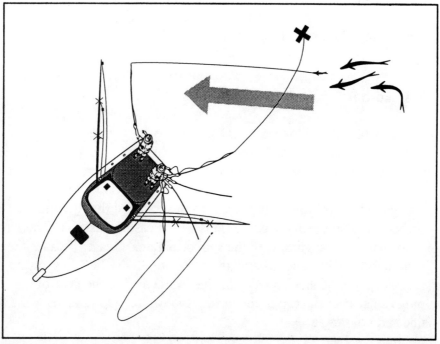

70. Casting with spin or plug tackle to tease dolphin from a dead boat

b. Rigging dead or live baits for teasing: To rig ballyhoo baits (dead or alive) use the same 15-footpiece of 150-pound mono-filament but tie in six 100-pound barrel swivels, one every 18 inches. A 10-inch piece of #8 stainless-steel wire is attached to the rear eye of each swivel with a haywire twist. The terminal end of the wire is bent up at a 90-degree angle to form a pin for attaching the ballyhoo bait.

Using several wraps around the wire ahead of the pin, secure a 6-inch piece of soft copper wrapping wire. After working the bait to make it swim properly run the wire from under the jaw, up through the head, and secure by wrapping the pin and bill of the ballyhoo with copper wire. Eighth-inch braided nylon is used for the main line from the swivel to the boat.

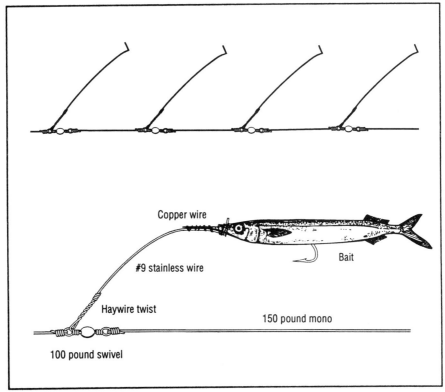

71. Ballyhoo trolling teaser

c. **Dead boat (drifting) casting teasers:** I recommend a Bagley Finger Mullet, MirrOlure 51M Sinker or a *7M 24 Floater* plug with all hooks removed for casting and teasing while drifting and fly casting to dolphin around flotsam and jetsam. I prefer these plugs because the towing eye is located directly on the nose. Other plugs with the towing eye located on top of the head will catch every piece of grass and fly line they get near. Larger lures can be used to increase casting distance, such as the Rapala 14 SM Magnum or the Bomber Long A Magnum.

Alterations must be made: Remove the hooks and remove the diving lip. The diving lip is plastic and breaks off and can be ground smooth so grass and fly lines don't catch on it. A short, 2-foot leader of 50-pound mono attached to the main line with a 60-pound barrel swivel can be used against chafing.

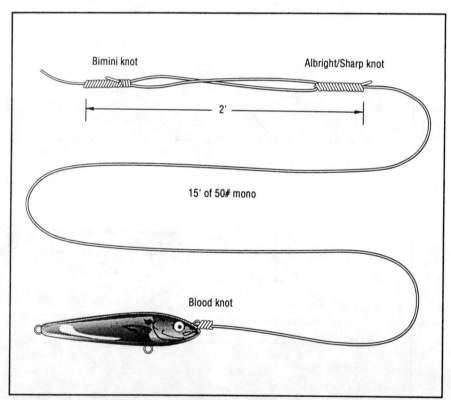

Bimini knot

Albright/Sharp knot

2'

15' of 50# mono

Blood knot

72. Rigging hookless baits for teasing dolphin within fly casting range.

d. **Using the kite for teasing dolphin:** The advantage of the kite is that surface baits, live or dead, can be lifted up out of the water and the fly presented to the gamefish. To tease dolphin, use a dedicated rod and reel to fly the kite, one with large guides so that a 60-pound-test swivel can pass through them and on to the reel. Capt. Bob Lewis manufactures kites for light wind, medium wind and heavy wind. I recommend light-wind kites for the small boater.

For teasing, you'll need a Black's marine release clip with the attaching bar removed. Pull off about 60 feet of kite line (50-pound test mono), cut it, and slide the modified release clip onto the terminal end of the line. Tie the two lines back together with a 60-pound-test barrel swivel. Reel the 60 feet of 50-pound mono line back on the kite reel. At the terminal end of the line attach the light-wind kite.

Fly the kite into the air. The kite line will run through the Black's release clip until it hits the swivel at the 60-foot mark. When it hits the swivel, stop and attach the fishing line with teasing bait in the release clip, then continue flying the kite out until the teasing bait is about 60 feet away from the boat. Adjust the fishing line so the bait skims across the surface of the water.

When a dolphin rises to the bait, you can tease it by lifting the bait in and out of the water. When the angler is ready to cast, pick up the bait and present the fly. Wind the kite line closer if needed to draw the fish in, or cast a hookless plug on spin or plug to excite and pull the fish closer for the presentation.

73. Teasing dolphin and presenting the fly using the kite.

G. "Setting Trolling Patterns"

1. Baits and lures

Normally, the pattern for trolling is the same for lures, baits or combinations of the two. It's important to stagger the baits so the area behind the boat is fully covered and lines are well-spaced so tangling doesn't occur when turning. (See *Illustration G-1* for a typical trolling pattern.)

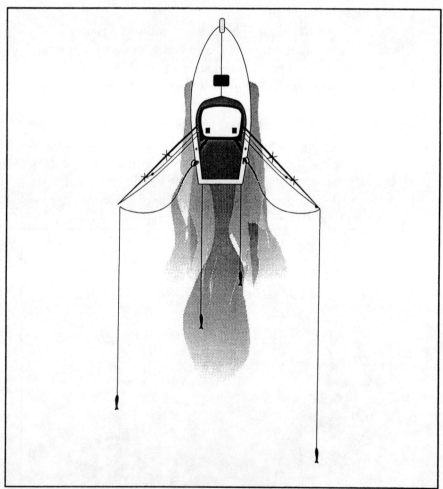

74. Typical trolling pattern with baits or lures.

2. Trolling pattern for sight-casting to dolphin

When the wind opposes the current, dolphin begin to tail, particularly on winds over 15 knots. To be successful with these fish you must sight them and cast a ballyhoo or flying fish on spin or plug tackle to the fish. Here is a trolling pattern to facilitate sight casting: Troll three lures/baits instead of the normal four – two in the outriggers and one in the center rigger up high and out of your way for casting from the cockpit. If you don't have a center rigger you might tie a release clip on the T-top. Otherwise, eliminate the center line and just use the riggers. When tailing dolphin are encountered, the angler can cast under the rigger along side the boat to the tailing fish. Occasionally dolphin will strike one of the trolling baits/lures or be attracted into the spread.

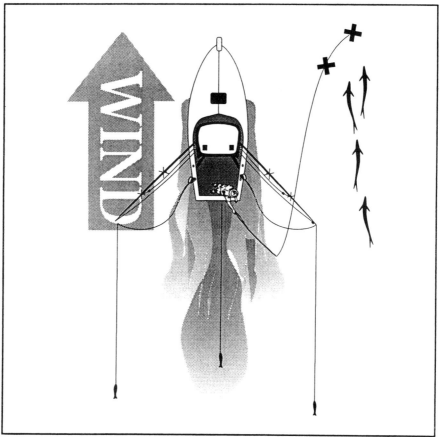

75. Sight casting to dolphin trolling pattern.

3. Dolphin on the deep-troll

The trolling pattern should be adjusted for trolling with a deep-troll so that the deep-troll bait/lure will surface near the outriggers after a hook-up or strike occurs. During northerly winds or upwelling currents, dolphin will usually strike the deep-troll first then others will follow the hooked fish to the surface. A properly positioned deep-troll and outriggers will bring additional strikes from excited dolphin following the hooked fish.

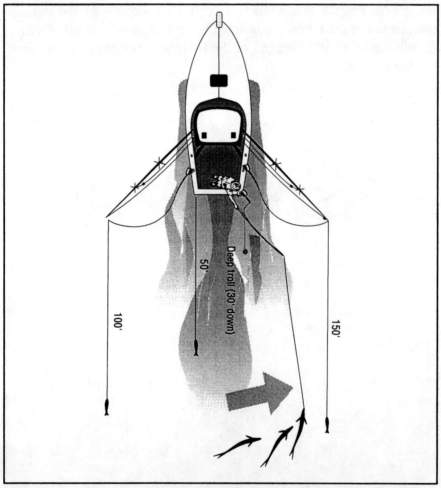

76. Proper positioning of the deep-troll and outrigger lines will bring additional strikes as the hooked dolphin brings others to the surface.

H. "Accessories"

1. Marker buoys to assist in relocating flotsam and jetsam

When dolphin schools are encountered on floating objects, a marker buoy should be thrown overboard to help relocate the spot. Marker buoys can be as simple as a white plastic jug with a 3-ounce sinker attached or a dive float and flag as shown below.

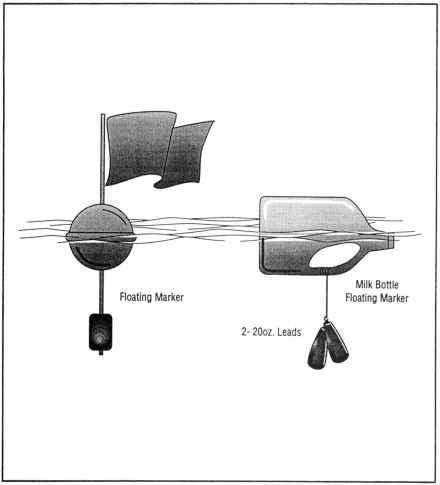

77. Two simple marker buoys for relocating flotsam and jetsam.

2. Gaffs

I recommend two gaffs for dolphin fishing: A long-handled gaff approximately 8 feet in length with a 6-inch stainless-steel hook for dolphin over 20 pounds and a shorter 3- to 5-foot gaff (depending on the freeboard of the boat) made of a fiberglass rod blank with a 2- or 3-inch stainless hook. This smaller, more streamlined gaff is great for dolphin under 20 pounds. A solid rod blank is stronger but the hollow glass rod blank will float if dropped overboard.

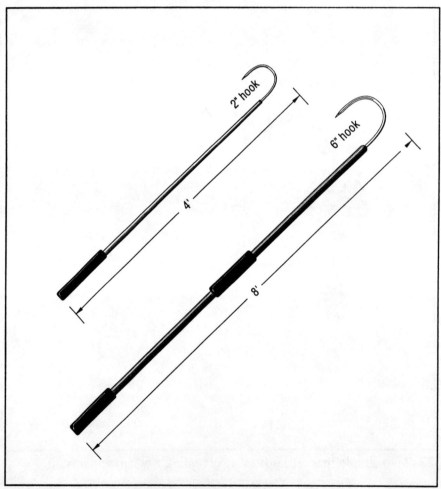

78. The selection of gaffs needed for dolphin.

3. Un-hooker

I highly recommend the un-hooker tool. Used in the northeast for a number of years with great success, it makes taking the hook out of a fish safe and easy. As you can see in the illustration, you hook the leader above the hook in the fish and slide the un-hooker down onto the shank of the hook pulling down on the leader and lifting and twisting on the un-hooker to release the hook.

79. Using the un-hooker, step one.

80. Using the un-hooker, step two

I. "Dolphin Fins"

Although the size and shape of the fins of common and pompano dolphin differ, the names remain the same. This chart should be used to identify the fins of the dolphin only. To distinguish the common dolphin from the pompano dolphin use the illustrations in Chapter One. To distinguish the male (bull) from the female (cow) refer to illustrations in Chapter Two.

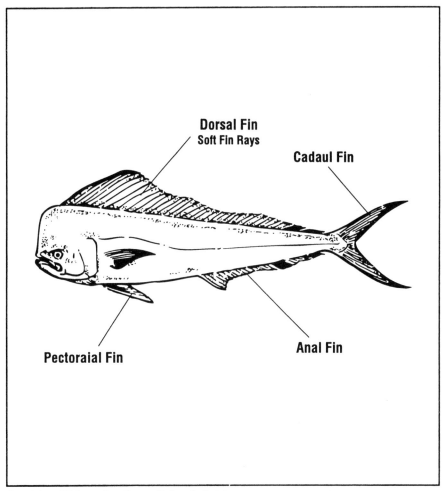

81. Identifying the fins of the dolphin.

Dolphin: **The Perfect Gamefish**

J. "Dolphin Fisherman's Crystal Ball"

Designed by Capt. Jim Sharpe the, "Dolphin Fisherman's Crystal Ball" wheel is a quick reference guide to the information contained in this book. It is water resistant and designed to be carried on the water. To use the quick reference wheel you simply enter the wind direction and moon phase for any fishing day and the quick reference wheel will predict dolphin feeding behavior and best method to catch them. It will also predict changes in the dolphin's feeding habits as the fishing day progresses as environmental factors change.

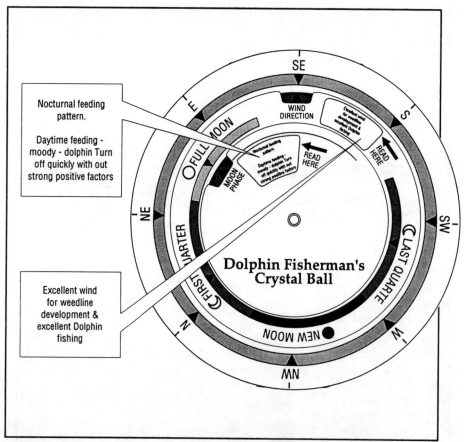

82. Dolphin Fisherman's Crystal Ball, designed by Capt. Jim Sharpe for quick reference.

K. "Recommended references"

- Fisherman's Knots, Rigs by Bob McNally
  Published by McNally Outdoor Productions, 1993

- *Fishing Tide Guide* by Florida Sportsman
  Wickstrom Publishers, 1997

- World Record Fishes, IGFA
  International Game Fish Association

- Birds of North America
  Western Publishing Company Inc., 1966

- NOAA Technical Report NMFS Circular 443: *Synopsis of the Biological Data on Dolphin-Fishes*
  National Marine Fisheries Service, U.S. Department of Commerce, April 1982

Glossary

A

Adult feeding school: Adult dolphin in the off-spawning cycle commonly comprised of mostly female fish ranging from 8 to 22 pounds.

Adult spawning school: Male and female fish schooling for the purpose of feeding and spawning.

Albright knot: Knot used to tie a leader onto a double line, used in wind-on leaders, originated by Captain Jimmy Albright.

Albright/Sharpe knot: Variation of the Albright knot, tied with the use of a paper clip to keep tight turns on the tag line and passed through the eye differently.

Anal fin: See *Illustration of fish and fin location, Appendix I*

Artificial lure or bait: Made from plastic, metal or wood. Designed to look like a baitfish when trolled or cast.

B

Baits: See *artificial, natural* or *cut*

Baitfish: Small fish, 2 to 6 inches in length, including: jacks, puffer, file, ballyhoo and flying fish.

Ballyhoo: A baitfish 10 to 12 inches in length found in the nearshore waters of Florida. Most common baitfish used by anglers.

Bimini twist: A knot used to form a double line, breaks at 100% of the line test and acts as a shock absorber to prevent line failure.

Bonito: Also called *little tunny*, a dark-meat tuna, recognized by light and dark-blue lines dorsally and seven black dots behind the gill plate.

Bonus year: A fishing season with larger-than-normal catches of dolphin. Occurs every three to five years .

Blackfin tuna: A tuna averaging 15 to 25 pounds. Dark blue back with long, black pectoral fins, gold bands along the sides and dark finlets; also see *tuna.*

Black noddy tern: Smaller than noddy tern, black color and slender bill. Feeds without diving. Swims under water to catch prey .

Blood knot: See *Sharpe's Blood Knot* and *Improved Blood Knot.*

Bright nights: Those three or four nights on the full moon when the nights are extremely bright

Bull dolphin: The male dolphin, generally larger and with a high vertical forehead.

C

Casting tackle: Spin or rotary-spool reels and rods specially designed for casting baits or lures.

Celsius: After A. Celsius (1701-1744). A temperature scale on which 0° is the freezing point and 100° is the boiling point of water.

Chicken dolphin: Common term in the Florida Keys for juvenile dolphin ranging from 4 to 6 pounds.

Chumming: Tossing small pieces of bait into the water to attract dolphin.

Chunking: See *chumming*.

Concave: Hollow and curved like the inside half of a hollow ball.

Conventional tackle: Rotary spool reels such as *GLS 25 Penn*, used for trolling not casting, which retrieve line as spool rotates. A lever is used to free-spool or release line. Also see *rotary spool reel*.

Convex: Curving outward like the surface of a sphere.

Copepods: Small crustaceans found in the ocean. The main diet of young dolphin.

Coastal tides: Inshore tides that interact with ocean currents extending offshore to 25 miles.

Coastal tide rips: Area of turbulence where ocean currents interact with coastal tides.

Color change: Area where murky inshore water meets and mixes with clear ocean water.

Common dolphin: *Coryphaena hippurus*, the more coastal, most common and larger of the two species, reaching 80 pounds or more.

Common tern: Has 30-inch wing span and short tail. Noticeably darker than the Roseate tern.

Counter currents: Inshore currents flowing in the opposite direction of strong offshore currents.

Cow dolphin: Female common dolphin, generally smaller than the bull (male), with a rounded, gently-sloping forehead.

Crustacean: Small crab-like animals. Also see *copepods*.

Cut bait: Small chunks of bait, such as one ballyhoo cut into six smaller pieces. Used for school dolphin.

D

Dead-boat casting: Fly casting from a drifting boat near flotsam.

Deep-troll: A reel with cable, release device and weight that allows fisherman to drop a trolling bait up to 100 feet below the surface; also called *downrigger*.

Dolphin: See *bull, cow, common* and *pompano*.

Dorsal fin: Fin located on the back of a fish; also see *Appendix I*.

Double-line: A line doubled by tying a Bimini twist or spider hitch knot. The double line acts as a shock absorber to prevent line failure under stress.

Downrigger: See *deep-troll*.

Drift fishing: Fishing while the boat drifts with the current and wind.

E

Eddies: Circular, spinning masses of water developed along the edges of currents.

El Niño: An erratic climate phenomenon in the tropics, caused by a warm-water current off the coast of Peru, affecting migrating and feeding fish.

Embolism: In some fish, a sudden change in depth can over-inflate the swim bladder and render the fish helpless at the surface.

Equator: An imaginary circle dividing the earth into the Northern Hemisphere and Southern Hemisphere.

Equatorial zone: An area extending from 20° south of the equator to 20° north of the equator.

F

Fall migration: See *migration*.

Fahrenheit: After G.D. Fahrenheit, 18th century physicist. A temperature scale on which 32° is the freezing point and 212° is the boiling point of water.

Feeding school: Dolphin schooling for the purpose of feeding. Generally comprised of 4- to 6-pound fish.

Fertilization: Uniting of sperm and egg in the water as dolphin swim side by side.

Flat line: Any line fished directly from the rod tip to the water while trolling; not in an outrigger or down rigger.

Flood tide: High tides with greater tidal volume occurring on the full moon.

Florida current: A part of the Gulf Stream current flowing close to the Florida coast.

Flotsam: Any number of objects found floating on the surface of the ocean including seaweed, boards, rope etc.; also see *jetsam*.

Fly tackle: Rod, reel, line and leaders used for fly fishing.

Fly leader: The butt section, line-class tippet and shock tippet.

Fly line: A weighted and tapered line used to cast a fly.

Fly: An artificial lure, hand tied with fur or feathers to look like baitfish.

Flying fish: Small baitfish with wing-like pectoral fins for gliding over the surface of the ocean, the preferred prey of adult dolphin.

Flying fish reflex: A reflex action of dolphin to turn and eat baitfish when they suddenly splash down in the water near the dolphin.

File fish: Small baitfish found around boards and sargassum sea weed; also see *Appendix: Baitfish*.

Fishing kite: A square kite flown on its own rod and reel with outrigger clips, used to elevate live or dead baits for fishing.

Frigate bird: See *man-o-war bird*.

G

Gaffer: Term used in the Florida Keys for dolphin large enough to gaff. Also see *slammer*.

Gaff: A rod or pole with a large barbless hook attached to the end, used to lift fish that are too heavy to lift with the leader.

Gannet: A marine bird with a 70-inch wing span, white wings with black tips. Feeds by diving from 50 feet or more into the water and swimming short distances to catch baitfish.

Greyhounding: Gamefish jumping repeatedly in a low arc across the surface of the water.

Gulf Stream: A current originating in the Florida Straits flowing northward along the east coast of the United States then northeast toward Europe.

Gray skies: Occur when a non-tropical, upper-level low pressure area moves into the area.

H

High tide: When the tide reaches its highest point on the incoming tide; also see *flood tide*.

I

Improved Sharpe's Blood Knot: Blood knot with tag end passed through larger loop for the finish, used to tie monofilament to the spool of a reel or secure hook, swivel, etc.

Incoming tide: A rising tide moving toward the high tide.

Isotherms: Areas of constant mean surface water temperatures.

J

Jack fish: Common baitfish, 2 to 6 inches in length, found around boards and seaweed; also see *Appendix, Baitfish*.

Jetsam: Variety of objects floating on the surface of the ocean; also see *flotsam*.

Jet stream: Any of several bands of high-velocity winds moving from west to east around the earth at altitudes of 8 to 10 miles.

Juvenile feeding schools: The first social order of dolphin life, dolphin from 2 to 6 pounds schooling for protection and feeding.

K

Kite: See *fishing kite*.

Kingfish: King mackerel. The largest of the mackerel family, reaching more than 60 pounds.

L

Larvae: The immature stage of development dolphin reach about 38 hours after the egg is fertilized.

Leader: A short monofilament line extending from the double line to the bait, also see: *wind on, trolling, sight-cast, light spin* or *fly leader.*

Line-class tippet: Leader of 2- to 20-pound-test line no shorter than 15 inches in length. Determines the line-class for fly fishing.

Live baiting: Fishing with live baitfish.

Lock jaw: Term used to describe the condition of a dolphin that will not bite.

Low-pressure systems: Areas of lower barometric pressure, including tropical low-pressure systems and non-tropical upper level low-pressure systems.

Low tide: When the tide reaches its lowest point on the out-going tide.

M

Man-o-war bird: Also called *frigate bird.* A very efficient glider with a 90-inch wing span, prominently crooked wings and forked tail. Feeds on surface baitfish but never dives into or lands on the water.

Marker buoy: A device used to mark and relocate a floating object where dolphin strikes occurred.

Meanders: Small, snake-like currents that wind off major currents such as the Gulf Stream.

Micro-chicken: A term used in the Florida Keys to describe very small dolphin – 2 to 4 pounds.

Migration: Movement of dolphin toward the equator in winter (fall migration) and away from the equator in summer (spring migration).

N

Natural bait: Rigged, dead baitfish such as ballyhoo, mullet or flying fish, as opposed to live or artificial bait.

Neap tide: Lower tides with greater tidal volume occurring around the new moon.

New moon: The dark moon, aligned between the earth and the sun, with its dark side to the earth. Dark nights.

Nocturnal feeding: Fish feeding at night.

Noddy tern: Common on Dry Tortugas, Florida. Dark body, white cap and wedge-shaped tail, not forked. Feeds without diving. Swims under water to catch prey.

O

Oceanic: Remaining far out at sea.

Offshore swivel knot: A knot used to tie a double line to a swivel; very strong and offers excellent abrasion quality.

Open window technique: Keeping one dolphin in the water, hooked, to attract the rest of the school.

Outgoing tide: A dropping tide flowing offshore until the low tide is reached.

Outrigger: Two long poles mounted on either side of a boat, used to separate lines and offer an automatic dropback to striking fish. Also called *rigger*.

P

Pectoral fin: Either of a pair of fins extending from the side of a fish, just behind the head. See *Appendix I*.

Phytoplankton: See *algae*.

Pompano Dolphin: *Coryphaena equiselis*, a smaller, more oceanic species (rarely weighing more than 8 pounds). A rare catch in coastal waters but common in the waters of Hawaii.

Pod: See *wolf pack*.

R

Rigger: See *outrigger*.

Rigging baits: Techniques used in rigging natural or artificial baits to swim like live fish.

Rigger clip: A device used to hold the fishing line up in the outrigger, releasing when a strike occurs.

Rigger line: Line with rigger clip, used to haul the fishing line up the outrigger. Also, a line fished from an outrigger.

Roseate tern: Wing span of 30 inches, a white forked tail and a black bill with red only at the base; also see *tern*.

Rotary spool reel: See *conventional tackle*.

Royal tern: Deeply forked tail, thick orange bill and slow wing beat. Found offshore; also see *tern*.

S

Sailfish: A large tropical marine fish with a large, sail-like dorsal fin and a sword-shaped upper jaw called a bill.

Sargassum: A yellow-brown algae that floats on the surface of the Atlantic; also called *seaweed*.

Salinity: The number of parts per thousand of salt dissolved in sea water, ranging from 28/1000 to 39/1000.

Sea Boots: A world-famous charter fishing boat owned and operated by Captain Jim Sharpe and his family on Summerland Key in the Florida Keys.

Sea horse: A small, semitropical marine fish with a slender tail, plated body, and a head resembling a horse.

Seaweed: See *Sargassum*.

School dolphin: See *schoolies*.

Schoolies: Small dolphin fish ranging from 6 to 12 pounds.

Schooling: A number of dolphin coming together for protection, feeding or spawning.

Scombroids: Family of jacks.

Sharpe's Blood knot: Knot used to tie a hook or a swivel onto a monofilament leader. Will not slip if tied correctly. When doubled to give more abrasion resistance, it's called a *tuna knot*.

Shiira-zuke fishery: A fishery off the coast of Japan where bamboo rafts are used to attract dolphin schools.

Shock tippet: Fly leader, no longer than 10 inches, used to prevent abrasion of the fly tippet.

Shoreward edge of the Gulf Stream: The part of the Gulf Stream current that is closest to shore.

Sight-casting: A technique that requires visually spotting the dolphin on the surface and casting a bait to the fish.

Skipjack tuna: A true tuna with bluish/purple back and white underside with seven lateral black stripes. Averages 12 to 14 pounds; also see *tuna*.

Slack tide: A short period at the change of the tide when the current is not flowing.

Slammer: A term used in the Florida Keys to describe a dolphin 16 pounds or larger.

Snap casting: A quick-delivery method of casting a fly.

Social order: The different levels of dolphin schooling assorted by sex and size; juvenile feeding, adult spawning, adult feeding and the wolf pack.

Soft rays: The dorsal spines that support fins in the dolphin are soft, not bony.

Sooty tern: Dark, sooty-colored tern with forked tail. Does not dive into the water but catches fish in flight or plucks them from the surface.

Southerly quadrant: From 90 degrees to 180 degrees on the compass.

Spawning school: Dolphin schooling for the purpose of spawning.

Spider hitch: A knot used to form a double line, not as strong as Bimini twist knot but quicker to tie. See *Bimini twist*.

Spin tackle: A casting reel with a bail spinning around the spool to retrieve line, opened to release line or cast.

Spring migration: See *migration.*

Straits of Florida: The area between the Bahama Islands, Cuba and the coast of Florida.

Squid: Cephalopod mollusks with a slender body and ten arms, two arms are longer and specialized for grasping.

Swim bladder: A gas-filled sac in the body cavity of most bony fishes, giving buoyancy to the body.

T

Tackle: See *troll, spin-cast* or *fly.*

Tail walking: A term used to describe a gamefish jumping across the surface with just its tail in the water.

Tailing: A term used to describe a fish swimming at the surface, usually with the tip of its tail exposed, using the circular movement of wave energy to propel it into the flow of a strong current.

Tailing conditions: A brisk wind opposing the direction of a strong current.

Teaser: Natural or artificial bait without hooks, used to lure gamefish to strike other baits.

Tern: Slender birds with long, narrow wings, forked tail and a pointed bill; also see *roseate, common, sooty* and *noddy tern*

Tide: Water rising and falling with the gravitational pull of the moon and sun.

Tidal rips: Areas along the edges of strong currents where the water ripples and swirls.

Tippet: See *shock tippet* or *line class tippet*

Trade winds: Predominately southeasterly winds of summer in the southern Atlantic and Florida Keys.

Tropical waters: The equatorial area of the ocean between the Tropic of Cancer and the Tropic of Capricorn.

Trolling: A method of fishing from a moving boat.

Trolling tackle: Rods and reels from 12- to 130-pound test used when trolling for gamefish.

Troll/tease: A technique used to lure gamefish to the boat and then cast light fishing tackle; also see *fly casting.*

Trolling patterns: The spacing of natural or artificial baits to attract the maximum number of strikes.

Trolling leaders: Leaders equipped with heavy lock swivels for changing baits during trolling; also see *wind-on leader.*

Tagging: Placing a numbered, metal or nylon identification dart into the back of a fish. An information card with corresponding number is filled out and sent to *National Marine Fisheries* giving date, size and location of tagging.

Tuna: An excellent eating gamefish; see also *yellowfin, blackfin, skipjack.*

Tuna knot: See *blood knot.*

U

Upwelling: Water from the bottom being forced to the surface by the action of current and wind.

V

Vertebrate: The large group of animals having a backbone, brain and skull.

Visual stimulation: Floating objects in the ocean give fish a navigational reference and focal point in an otherwise optical void.

W

Wahoo: Similar to the kingfish and mackerels, dark blue dorsally with silver and blue vertical stripes along sides. Can be distinguished from the kingfish by vertical stripes and large caudal peduncle. Excellent fighter.

Weed fish: A small fish found in the waters off southeastern Tasmania. *Heteroclinus* species.

Weedline: Sargassum, (yellow-brown algae) lined up in long, straight rows by the interaction of wind and currents.

White egret: A large, white, wading bird common to the southeastern United States. Migrates across the Florida Straits.

Wind-on leader: A series of double line, leader and knots designed to be wound through guides and onto the reel. Eliminates hand-pulling long leaders.

Wolf pack: Three to six dolphin of 20 to 40 pounds feeding together, the final stage in the social order of dolphin.

Y

Yellowfin tuna: Averages 100 to 200 pounds, dark blue on back, golden bands along sides. Young tunas can have white spots on belly. Dorsal and anal fins can be elongated. Distinguished from *blackfin* by bright yellow finlets and fins.

Index

ORDER FORM

To order additional copies of *"Dolphin: The Perfect Gamefish"*, by Captain Jim Sharpe, send a check or money order for **$45.95** for each book. This includes tax, shipping, and handling. Please indicate the number of books you want to order:

    1 copy.................................$ 45.95
    2 copies..............................$ 91.90
    3 copies..............................$137.85
    4 copies..............................$183.80
    5 copies..............................$229.75
    6 copies or more will receive discount. Call for more information.

To order using all major credit cards: Fill out the form below and mail or fax to:

The Fisherman's International Publishing House
P.O. Box 421203 Summerland Key, FL 33042-1203

Ship To:
Name ———————————————————————

Street ———————————————————————

    ———————————————————————

City ————————————— State ———— Zip————

I authorize The Fisherman's International Publishing House to bill

$ ——————— to my:

MasterCard ☐   Visa ☐   American Express ☐   Discover ☐

Credit Card # ———————————————————

Expiration Date ——————————————

Signature ——————————————————

Fill in the amount with credit card number, expiration date and your signature then fax to: **305-872-0780**
Or mail to:

The Fisherman's International Publishing House
P.O. Box 421203 Summerland Key, FL 33042-1203

For more information call 800-238-1746.

ORDER FORM

To order Captain Jim Sharpe's quick reference wheel the *"Dolphin Fisherman's Crystal Ball"* send a check or money order for **$12.95** this includes tax, shipping, and handling. Please indicate the number of wheels you want to order.

1 wheel........................$ 12.95
2 wheels......................$ 25.90
3 wheels......................$ 38.85
4 wheels......................$ 51.80
5 wheels......................$ 64.75
6 wheels or more will receive discount. Call for more information.

To order using all major credit cards: Fill out the form below and mail or fax to:

The Fisherman's International Publishing House
P.O. Box 421203 Summerland Key, FL 33042-1203

Ship To:

Name _____

Street _____

_____

City _____ State _____ Zip_____

I authorize The Fisherman's International Publishing House to bill

$ _____ to my:

MasterCard ☐   Visa ☐   American Express ☐   Discover ☐

Credit Card # _____

Expiration Date _____

Signature _____

Fill in the amount with credit card number, expiration date and your signature then fax to: **305-872-0780**
Or mail to:

The Fisherman's International Publishing House
P.O. Box 421203 Summerland Key, FL 33042-1203

For more information call 800-238-1746.

ORDER FORM

Captain Jim has produced a "How To Video" on dolphin fishing. Edited and narrated by the author this fifty-eight minute video captures the color and excitement of dolphin fishing in the Gulfstream off the Florida Keys while offering a number of helpful tips to dolphin fishermen. To order Captain Jim Sharpe's *"How to Catch Dolphin"* video send a check or money order for **$29.95** this includes tax, shipping and handling.

Please indicate the number of video's you want to order.

1 video....................29.95
2 videos..................49.90 10 dollar discount
3 videos..................89.85 20 dollar discount
4 videos or more 30% discount

To order using all major credit cards: Fill out the form below and mail or fax to:

**The Fisherman's International Publishing House
P.O. Box 421203 Summerland Key, FL 33042-1203**

Ship To:
Name _____

Street _____

_____

City _____ State _____ Zip_____

I authorize The Fisherman's International Publishing House to bill

$ _____ to my:

MasterCard ☐   Visa ☐   American Express ☐   Discover ☐

Credit Card #_____

Expiration Date _____

Signature _____

Fill in the amount with credit card number, expiration date and your signature then fax to: **305-872-0780**
Or mail to:

**The Fisherman's International Publishing House
P.O. Box 421203 Summerland Key, FL 33042-1203**

For more information call 800-238-1746.